Praise for *Winning Roles for Career-Minded Women*

"This book provides both clear guides for the roles of women at work and insightful suggestions for changing problematic thinking and behavior to maximize work, efficiency, and satisfaction."

—Aaron T. Beck, M.D., University Professor of Psychiatry, University of Pennsylvania

"This is the most practical tool I've ever seen for understanding why and how one drives personal outcomes in the business environment—and what to do to maximize one's potential to succeed. It is a treasure trove of insight at the most personal level."

—Sandra D. Kresch, Partner, Entertainment and Media Strategy Practice, PricewaterhouseCoopers LLP

"This book presents important new insights into why women function as they do in their respective roles at work. Its clarity and practical suggestions for change enhance its appeal as a useful guide for women."

—John E. Ryan, Home Office Learning & Development Manager, The TJX Companies, Inc.

"What better tandem to explore the effect of family-generated roles that women play in their careers than a daughter-and-mother team who are both professional psychologists! The authors show the astute reader how to transcend her well-worn familial habits, and to broaden her repertoire—both in terms of her self-perceptions and in how she navigates the world of work and achievement. An important contribution to women's wellness!"

—Cory F. Newman, Ph.D., Clinical Director, Center for Cognitive Therapy, University of Pennsylvania School of Medicine

"Because it depicts both the hazards of various roles in the workplace and the successful resolution to the challenges, *Winning Roles for Career-Minded Women* is a valuable addition to the bookshelf of both the individual looking for personal understanding and the professional counselor providing guidance to a client."

—Jane McGarrahan, Ph.D., Director, Graduate Program in Counseling Psychology, Holy Family College

"This book is great reading for anyone looking to understand the issues underlying the advancement and retention of women in business."

—Laurie Lawsky, Regional Human Resources Director

WINNING ROLES
FOR CAREER-MINDED WOMEN

WINNING ROLES
FOR CAREER-MINDED WOMEN

Understanding the Roles We Learned as Girls and How to Change Them for Success at Work

Binnie Shusman Kafrissen and Fran Shusman

Foreword by Joanna Smith Bers

Editorial Director of YouDecide.com
and former Editor of *Success* magazine

Davies-Black Publishing
Palo Alto, California

OUACHITA TECHNICAL COLLEGE

Published by Davies-Black Publishing, an imprint of Consulting Psychologists Press, Inc., 3803 East Bayshore Road, Palo Alto, CA 94303; 800-624-1765

Special discounts on bulk quantities of Davies-Black books are available to corporations, professional associations, and other organizations. For details, contact the Director of Book Sales at Davies-Black Publishing, 3803 East Bayshore Road, Palo Alto, CA 94303; 650-691-9123; fax 650-623-9271.

04 03 02 01 00   10 9 8 7 6 5 4 3 2 1
Printed in the United States of America

Library of Congress Cataloging-in-Publication Data

Kafrissen, Binnie Shusman
  Winning roles for career-minded women : understanding the roles we learned as girls and how to change them for success at work / Binnie Shusman Kafrissen and Fran Shusman.
  —1st ed.
        p.   cm.
  Includes bibliographical references and index.
  ISBN 0-89106-146-0 (pbk.)
  1. Women—Psychology. 2. Achievement motivation in women.
  3. Sex role. 4. Women—Social conditions. I. Shusman, Fran

HQ1206 .K34 2000
158.1′083—dc21
                                        00-043181

FIRST EDITION
First printing 2000

CONTENTS

Foreword   ix
Joanna Smith Bers

Preface   xi

About the Authors   xiii

Introduction   xv

PART ONE
The Roles We Play   1

1 Roles in the Family   3

2 Role of the Peacekeeper   19

3 Role of the Maverick   31

4 Role of the Pleaser   43

5 Role of the Caregiver   55

6 Role of the Survivor   67

7 Role of the Entrepreneur   79

8 Comparing and Combining Roles   91

PART TWO
Changing Our Roles to Succeed at Work   101

9 Understanding Roles in the Workplace   103

10 Changing the Way We Think   123

11 Changing the Way We Act   143

12 Creating Our Future   159

References   167

Index   169

FOREWORD

Joanna Smith Bers

When I finished *Winning Roles for Career-Minded Women,* I thought about all the conversations, self-examinations, and discoveries that had resulted from reading it. I began to hear the faint echo of a distant voice. The longer I thought, the louder the voice became until I could hear the words booming out of my memory: "You can, and you will!"

It was a warm afternoon in June and I was sitting in the grassy meadow behind my high school. At first there was silence, and then I heard a voice electrify the air, saying, "You can, and you will." The man who so assuredly spoke those words was none other than author Stephen King. That's right, the guy who has spun such horrifying tales as *Carrie* and *Pet Sematary* was gushing with this optimistic charge. So what was he doing on the lawn of my high school promising me success? He was delivering a spectacular commencement address. His message: You are not going to win the lottery. No one is going to tap you on the head with a magic wand and make all your dreams come true. It is up to you to make your life into what you want it to be. You can, and you will.

King's optimism that afternoon stemmed from his ongoing belief that, like him, we all possess certain talents and skills that will enable us to achieve our goals. Before he became a best-selling author, Stephen King used to stroll through bookstores thumbing through various volumes and thinking, "I could write something better than this." And guess what? He could and did.

It was King's appreciation for his talent and his willingness to harness it that enabled him to succeed. He knew what his strengths were and he didn't let weaknesses, such as self-doubt, get the better of him. But how many of us are so aware of our gifts and so able to overcome our insecurities?

In *Winning Roles for Career-Minded Women,* authors Binnie Shusman Kafrissen and Fran Shusman help readers identify their character strengths and weaknesses so that they, like King, can unequivocally pursue success. The authors hold up a mirror so that women can reflect on their lives and their deepest relationships to find a clearer understanding of who they are, why they behave the way they do, and how they can harness the best parts of themselves to achieve their goals and overcome any obstacles.

By examining women's most formative relationships, those with their families, Kafrissen and Shusman enable women to see the roles they've been playing all their lives, the roles they have taken on to survive or thrive in any situation or setting, including the workplace.

As *Winning Roles for Career-Minded Women* makes clear, once you are able to recognize the roles you play and the positive and negative consequences of your behavior at work, you can begin to modulate your behavior to achieve your goals and overcome the obstacles to your success. You can, and you will.

Joanna Smith Bers is Editorial Director of YouDecide.com and the former Editor of *Success* magazine.

PREFACE

Everyone said that our second book would be about what it is like to write a book with your daughter/mother. We are happy to report that we are still on speaking terms, and in all seriousness we have thoroughly appreciated this time to relate to each other as professionals as well as to further enhance our mother-daughter relationship. We are lucky. We have always been close, but working together on the book took that closeness to a whole new level. We now look forward to future collaborations as a mother-daughter team.

We wrote this book for women of all ages who seek to understand the impact their personal development has had on their professional life. *Winning Roles for Career-Minded Women* identifies the developmental and organizational issues that affect women, providing suggestions and exercises to help them find solutions. We encourage you to be an active participant as you read it, and subsequently in your life. It is our hope that you will take away from the book a clear understanding of how and why you function as you do in the workplace.

This work is a truly collaborative effort. We would like to thank the staff of Davies-Black Publishing for their belief in this book and their continual guidance. We extend our appreciation to Melinda Adams Merino for her support, encouragement, and understanding, and for patiently guiding us through the writing process. And we offer a very special thank you to our editor, Alan Shrader, whose direct and concise suggestions enabled us to see this book through to completion.

We would also like to thank all the women who shared their stories with us. Their enthusiasm was reflected in their desire and willingness to contact their friends and colleagues to be interviewed for this book. These busy women gave freely of their time, and without their cooperation this work would not have been possible. Their insights and experiences have been essential to the process of identifying the roles women play at work.

On a personal note, we would like to thank our extended family for all of their love, encouragement, and support during this project. A very special thankyou goes to the most important people in our lives, our husbands, Samuel Kafrissen and Gene Shusman. We would like to thank them for their understanding when our interviewing and writing commitments kept us from always being there for them. Their constant support and understanding has kept us going in the most difficult of times. They have given us the most precious of all gifts, the encouragement and freedom to fulfill our potential as women.

ABOUT THE AUTHORS

Binnie Shusman Kafrissen, Ph.D., is an organizational psychologist and president of The Delancey Group, an organization development consulting firm. She works with Fortune 500 corporations on issues such as leadership development, retention of women in the workforce, establishment of women's networking groups, executive coaching, and organization design and development. Her clients have included Citibank, Digital Equipment Corporation, Disney, General Electric, Pricewaterhouse-Coopers, Prudential Insurance, and Rosenbluth International. Formerly, Kafrissen was the manager of Leadership and Organizational Development at Pricewaterhouse-Coopers. She lives with her husband in Philadelphia.

Fran Shusman, Ph.D., is a licensed counseling psychologist in private practice and a clinical associate at the Center for Cognitive Therapy at the University of Pennsylvania. She is vice president of The Delancey Group. In her clinical work, she specializes in the treatment of depression and anxiety and has helped women deal with personal and professional issues that significantly affect the quality of their lives. She also provides services for a variety of companies through employee assistance programs. Shusman is clinical supervisor and mentor for other psychologists in the Department of Psychiatry at the University of Pennsylvania. She also has taught graduate-level psychology courses at Temple University in Philadelphia. She is the mother of three grown children and lives with her husband in Philadelphia.

INTRODUCTION

Winning Roles for Career-Minded Women explores the roles women play at work and the ways in which their development and organizational dynamics combine to create those roles. The goal of this book is to help women understand why they function as they do in their professional lives and to guide them in changing their behavior if they feel it is necessary or desirable to do so. In this book, we will examine women's development and how it affects their success in the workplace. We believe that when women understand why they think and act as they do, they will be able to redefine themselves, consolidate their strengths, and apply those strengths in all areas of their lives. We will also discuss organizational approaches that we believe will enable companies to utilize the untapped strengths of their female workforce.

Assuming that a woman's development has an impact on her behavior at work, we became interested in how societal and developmental issues contribute to professional self-concept and interactional style. We decided to interpret female behavior in the workplace as a function of development, theorizing that the roles women assume within their own families as children and young adults lay the groundwork for their adult professional roles. In other words, our current behavior frequently arises out of long-held beliefs about ourselves. We have included self-help exercises throughout this book to help you examine your beliefs about yourself.

Cognitive Therapy can assist in clearing away the distorted beliefs that may prevent you from reaching your maximum level of effectiveness. It is based on the assumption that your thoughts affect how you feel and consequently how you behave (Beck, 1976). For example, if you believe that you are not as smart and competent as your coworker, you will probably be anxious during meetings and hesitate to speak up, which may adversely affect your ability to promote yourself within your company. If, however, you could dispute this negative belief in your incompetence by reminding yourself of the good feedback you have received from your boss as well as all the creative solutions you have proposed, you will be more confident and express yourself more readily. In this book, you will learn to identify what you are telling yourself and to analyze these thoughts objectively. When we examine our thoughts, we're often able to recognize the distortions in our thinking and achieve a different perspective. The exercises in this book will help you understand how your beliefs about yourself may actually be sabotaging your attempts to be successful.

Over the years, we have compared notes about our respective disciplines and consistently found that collaboration has been helpful to our respective clients. This collaboration was the foundation for our book. We are psychologists who specialize in two different areas. Binnie is an organizational psychologist who has consulted for several Fortune 500 companies on issues such as organizational development and design, employee satisfaction, women in the workplace, training and development, and management and leadership development. She has worked extensively with women to develop both their leadership styles and their ability to encourage future leaders. In addition to consulting on external organizational change, Binnie has served as an internal organizational psychologist for Prudential, Rosenbluth International, and PricewaterhouseCoopers. Fran is a licensed psychologist in private practice in Philadelphia as well as a clinical associate at the Center for Cognitive Therapy at the University of Pennsylvania.

She specializes in Cognitive Therapy for the treatment of depression, anxiety, and relationship issues. She has been interested primarily in helping women to redefine themselves by recognizing their strengths and evaluating the distorted beliefs that have restricted them to unfulfilling roles.

We are not researchers or scientists in the academic sense. We are two women who have conducted psychological research in clinical and organizational settings and are applying what we've learned from our respective workplaces. We decided to give voice to the conversations we have had with friends and colleagues—over coffee and over dinner, in the ladies' room or in the shopping center, at the beach and on the phone. We have combined our research, conversations, interviews, and work experiences in this book to share what we have learned with you.

In an effort to make this book meaningful to you, the reader, we interviewed women from a variety of backgrounds in hopes of gathering and sharing information about women's conceptions of themselves and how these ideas affect their professional lives. We included excerpts from those interviews in order to provide a realistic picture of the issues we are discussing. We interviewed thirty women between the ages of twenty-three and sixty-five. Women at staff, middle management, and executive management levels were included in the interview sample and represent a variety of industries, managerial and nonmanagerial ranks, and ages. Educational levels vary as well, ranging from those who are high school graduates to those with undergraduate and graduate degrees. The women we interviewed are also highly diverse with regard to marital status and family history. To maintain confidentiality, we created composites of the interviewees to exemplify various roles.

While conducting these interviews and comparing notes, we identified themes and patterns of behavior that led us to formulate the different roles. It became apparent that the roles we assume early on within the family are eventually played out in the workplace. This led us to think of the family as the first organization, the one in which we all learn to function. The roles we play in the familial organization, which we develop as a means of coping with various family dynamics, lay the foundation for workplace behaviors. Over time, we become very adept at our particular style of functioning, and it shapes our behavior as well as our understanding of the world around us.

The roles we have identified in this book are in no way the only ones that exist, nor does everyone fit a single delineated role. Many people exhibit characteristics from a variety of roles; however, upon close examination, you may find that one role describes your behavior better than the others. By introducing you to a variety of roles, our intent is to guide you to a greater understanding of why you function the way you do. Throughout this book, we will explore how the various role behaviors help or hinder you in the workplace. We hope the information and exercises presented in this book will assist you in developing your own winning role for success.

PART ONE

THE ROLES WE PLAY

1 ROLES IN THE FAMILY

Once upon a time, there were six little girls. One little girl, named Lisa, lived in a suburban neighborhood with her parents, older sister, younger sister, and younger brother. Lisa was a happy, outgoing, and confident child. Her older sister, however, was unhappy and rebellious, which led to much friction in the home. It was upsetting for Lisa to see members of her family angry with one another. She was afraid that if she didn't do something, the tension would erupt into conflict. So she took it upon herself to make sure everything functioned smoothly in her family; she was the stabilizer. She says, "My role was to make everything okay." She did this by distracting the other family members; she clowned around and told jokes and entertaining stories to keep peace in the family. Lisa assumed the role of the **Peacekeeper.**

The second little girl, Jane, grew up in a large metropolitan city. Jane lived with her parents and younger sister. Jane was a fiercely independent child with a clear vision of what her life should be. She states, "I decided that I could never compete with my mother or anybody else on the femininity front, so therefore I had to do something else. I had to be bright, I had to be rebellious, and I think I was. I wasn't rebellious in the sense of breaking rules and getting into trouble; I was rebellious in the sense that I believed I knew what was best for me, and I followed that path." She has always been her own person and intuitively knows what is right for her. To her parents, her refusal to go along with their vision of what her life should be appeared threatening and rebellious. In taking on the role of the difficult child, Jane became the **Maverick.**

The third little girl, Ilene, grew up in a rural setting. Ilene lived with her parents and two younger sisters. Ilene was the good one, or as her sister called her, "Goody Two-Shoes." As a child, she observed how upset her father became when even the smallest things did not go his way. Ilene also noticed how her mother neglected her own needs to meet the needs of her husband and prevent him from becoming upset. She quickly learned this behavior. She was respectful, obedient, and followed the rules. Ilene never talked back to her parents and went to great lengths to make everyone in the family happy. She was so anxious to please them that she never developed or expressed any of her own thoughts and opinions. Ilene's role was that of the **Pleaser.**

The fourth little girl, Rachel, grew up in a suburban community with her mother, older brother, and younger sister. Her parents divorced when she was eight years old. She lived with her mother and saw her father periodically. After the divorce, her mother grew depressed and withdrawn. Eventually she became bedridden and was unable to take care of the children and the household. All these responsibilities fell to Rachel. At a very young age, when other girls were playing and just being kids, Rachel took on an adult role. Rachel assumed the role of the **Caregiver.**

The fifth little girl, Kate, grew up in a small town with her mother, father, and older brother. Kate was a shy and quiet little girl. School was especially difficult for her. Although she tried very hard, she usually did poorly on tests and written assignments. Her lack of academic success contrasted unfavorably with her brother's scholastic achievements. Kate was continually chastised and punished by her parents and teachers for what they perceived as her lack of interest and effort. Gradually,

Kate became more and more withdrawn and easily overwhelmed by the demands placed upon her. After several years, Kate was diagnosed with a learning disability, which was the reason for her problems in school. Despite this new awareness of what was causing her problems, Kate continued to believe that she was powerless and that the only way to deal with difficult situations was to withdraw. Kate assumed the role of the **Survivor.**

The sixth little girl, Jean, grew up in a small town. Jean lived with her mother, father, and younger sister. Jean was a strong, independent, and extremely active child. Although she loved and admired both of her parents, she identified with the unfettered spirit and adventurous life of her father, an engineer and inventor. Dad supported and encouraged her, and she took every opportunity to learn, try new things, and achieve. Her family was poor, and as a child she demonstrated her entrepreneurial talents by setting up a business and selling apples from the tree in her backyard. She distinguished herself in school and was the first woman to attend an all-male business college. While her sister followed her mother's role as a typically feminine and loving housewife, Jean pushed herself to succeed and overcome all obstacles. Jean assumed the role of the **Entrepreneur.**

Each member of a family assumes a role, and that role is both influenced by and a reaction to the roles played by other family members. For example, in the first story, Lisa the Peacekeeper was reacting to the turmoil created by her sibling, who had taken the role of the Maverick. In the second story, Jane the Maverick battled with her parents to be the person she believed she had to be. Meanwhile, to avoid conflict with their parents, Jane's younger sister became a Pleaser, "a social, pretty, cheerleader type" who focused on her appearance, not on her abilities. In the third story, Ilene the Pleaser recalls that her youngest sister was the difficult child, constantly creating turmoil in the family. But Ilene's sister recently told her that she felt she could never compete with Ilene, who was so good and always trying to do what everyone wanted her to do, so she went in the opposite direction and became a Maverick. In the fourth story, Rachel became the Caregiver after seeing her mother fall into the role of victim after her divorce. In the fifth story, Kate became the Survivor in response to continual criticism over her poor grades. In the sixth story, Jean the Entrepreneur broke with the traditional female behavior of her time; she was more interested in pursuing a career in business than in acquiring domestic skills. Her mother was often distressed by Jean's lack of interest in cooking and sewing. Jean's younger sister observed this and took on the role of the Pleaser by showing an interest in the more traditional female activities. We cite these examples to show how the various roles affect one another.

And the six little girls grew up. They are now women with adult professional and personal relationships. In talking about their lives, we saw that the roles women assume as adults often mirror the ones they played in their families when they were children. Think about it. How did you react to your mom and dad? Do you see any connection in the way you respond to your boss? How did you interact with your brothers or sisters? Do you see any similarities in your interactions with coworkers? As children, we learned how to interact with authority figures, take criticism, get attention, ask for what we want, negotiate, and speak up for ourselves. We also learned the consequences of these actions by seeing how other people reacted to us.

After identifying the connection between the workplace and the family, we began to think of the family as the first, or original, organization. It is where we learn the rules of hierarchy, structure, culture, power, and interaction with others. We carry these experiences and learned behaviors with us into our adult lives, where they form the basis for the roles we play at home and at work. A look at the adult experiences of the six little girls illustrates the manner in which this happens.

Lisa the Peacekeeper

Lisa is a thirty-nine-year-old human resources executive who works for a large, professional services firm. She is married and has two children. As a child, Lisa saw herself as the person who had to make everything okay; she functioned as a stabilizing force in her family. She continued this role into her marriage. Lisa states, "I am the stable force in my relationship with my husband. He's the kind of person who is all over the place, and I'm the stable one."

"As a child, I wanted my sister to be happy and get along with my parents. It's interesting that I was doing that then and I'm doing the same thing now in a group communication process, trying to ensure that everyone in the group gets along and works as a team. I am the stable force in this environment because there are all these members of my group who are dealing with a million things, and I am the stabilizing center." Lisa—a Peacekeeper

Lisa was a confident child who took on the task of stabilizing her family. In accepting this role, she was influenced primarily by concern about her older sister, an unhappy child who was creating friction in the family. Lisa wanted everyone in her family to get along and be happy. She recognizes the similarities between her behavior as a child and the behavior she currently displays as an employee of a large organization. Lisa continually tries to create a harmonious environment at work.

Jane the Maverick

Jane is a fifty-five-year-old partner in a large, international consulting firm that specializes in strategic planning for the entertainment industry. She is married and has no children. Jane struggled to define herself, declare her independence, and find her own path. She brought her individualistic approach to her decision regarding marriage and children. She chose not to get married until she had moved to New York City, established herself in her career, and been on her own for a while. She then married but quickly divorced. Eventually, she remarried but decided to hold off on having children. She states, "I grew up in consulting at a time when it didn't seem possible to have children and the kind of career I wanted at the same time."

Jane was always very independent and intuitively knew what was right for her. She was a strong-willed child who refused to go along with her parents' vision of what her life should be and instead charted her own course and stuck to it. She has known from childhood that she wanted to be in control of her life.

The issues of control and independence have carried over into Jane's professional life. She recognizes the similarities between her behavior as a child and her current behavior in the workplace. The choices she has made in terms of work have arisen out of her need for independence and control. It's always been difficult for her to deal with authority figures and follow other people's rules without question. As a result, she sought out a work environment that allows her to function independently.

> "One of the messages I received early on was that economic dependence was incompatible with independence. If I really wanted to be in control of my life, I had to be in a position to take care of myself." **Jane—a Maverick**

Ilene the Pleaser

Ilene is a forty-four-year-old assistant vice president at a financial services company. She is married and has three children. Ilene learned at an early age to subordinate her needs to those of the people around her in exchange for their affection and approval. She learned her role well and brought it with her into all areas of her life. When she married, she automatically slipped into the role of the Pleaser and made the needs of her husband a priority. Her lack of individual development continued as she focused her energies on pleasing everyone in her newly extended family. The arrival of her children made the process harder, as each member of her family had a different opinion about how she should be raising her children and what she should be doing with her life. She states, "I eventually realized that in trying to please everyone, I was not pleasing anyone, especially myself. I became depressed, and in order to come out of the depression, I had to make some changes."

Ilene was quiet, obedient, and respectful of others. She learned at an early age that she would receive positive attention from family members, especially her father, by doing what they wanted her to do. She is now working for a company that reminds her of her family, with a dominant male figure who directs the activities of those who are under his supervision. Her need to please others, especially authority figures, has carried over into her work life.

Ilene's desire for the affection and approval of coworkers and especially of those in positions of authority overrides her own thoughts about what she needs and what is good for her.

Rachel the Caregiver

Rachel is a thirty-year-old sales manager who works for a midsize insurance company. She is married and has one child. Early in life, Rachel took on the adult role of caring for her older brother, younger sister, and mother after her parents' divorce. She didn't have the chance to enjoy the carefree attitudes of childhood and developed into an overly responsible adult who takes charge in most of her relationships. She maintains this caregiving role in her marriage. Her husband can't decide on what career to pursue and has been exploring various options, so Rachel is the strong, responsible one and has become the dominant partner in the relationship.

Rachel spent her childhood taking care of her mother, brother, and sister, a stressful and difficult role. When she was growing up, she always felt she was the glue holding the family together. Rachel has brought many of her early caregiving traits into her professional life, where she functions as the mother figure and looks after the others.

Like many who assume the role of Caregiver, Rachel is frequently stressed and accepts multiple responsibilities. She is just beginning to learn the importance of setting limits and how and when to say "no."

Kate the Survivor

Kate is a twenty-eight-year-old administrative assistant in a large, information technology company. She is single. Kate, who believes she is powerless, brings this view of herself into all her relationships. She is continually attracted to men who are demanding and hard to please and who insist on exercising control over everything. In all of her relationships, both romantic and platonic, she allows people to push her around, criticize her, and take advantage of her. Kate was a shy and quiet child with an undiagnosed learning disability who was constantly criticized by her parents, teachers, and friends for her poor performance in school. As a result, she developed a low opinion of herself and relinquished any sense of power and control in her life. She responded to difficult situations by withdrawing. Although her problems in school were later resolved, Kate's self-concept didn't change, and she continues to play the role of the victim in her adult relationships.

Kate is an administrative assistant to a very demanding boss. She has many responsibilities and works long hours to fulfill them. The company employs few women and encourages competition among its employees. Kate has carried her survivor role into the workplace.

"As a woman in a predominantly male company, I believe that I have little or no power to change the way things work here. I do my best, but it never seems to be good enough. I tell myself that I just have to work harder and tolerate it because I need a job."

Kate—a Survivor

Jean the Entrepreneur

Jean is the fifty-eight-year-old founder and CEO of a home health-care agency. She is married and has three children. Jean, who admired the spirit and excitement of her father's life, let nothing stand in her way—as a young girl, when she was trying to get the best education she could, and as an adult, as she worked hard to establish herself in various endeavors. Her dedication to helping people, her drive to succeed, and her ability to overcome all obstacles by remaining focused on her goals has made her a very successful entrepreneur. She started her

> "I'm driven, focused, success-oriented, a workaholic, impatient, and tireless. I guess I summarize it by saying that I'm in overdrive. I don't have hobbies because work is my hobby. I've given up everything to make a success of my business." **Jean—an Entrepreneur**

own business in 1982, providing caregivers to people in their homes, and despite the effects of multiple sclerosis, she has worked tirelessly to develop her company, which now boasts forty-seven offices.

Jean was a strong, independent, and adventurous child. Although she grew up at a time when gender roles were clearly defined, she refused to be limited by societal dictates or economic conditions. She viewed the obstacles in her path as problems to be solved and never allowed them to prevent her from reaching her goal. Jean decided to reenter the business world after marrying and raising her children. True to her philosophy, which considers obstacles as problems in need of solutions, she started her own business when she realized that no one would hire her because she was suffering from multiple sclerosis. A determined, intelligent woman, Jean understood that the corporate world was not a culture that accepted individuals with physical limitations.

Identifying Your Role

As we examine the stories of these women, we can see the impact of their respective childhood experiences upon their adult lives. They have made choices that conform to the beliefs they developed about themselves within their families. They all know which roles they should play in the different relationships that make up their lives, and they are able to identify similarities between the roles they assumed in their families and the roles they currently maintain.

The six roles we have described are in no way the only ones that exist in the family or in the workplace. Our intention has been to introduce you to a sample of various roles with which you may identify. As you read over the different role characteristics, you may recognize several of them in your own behavior. If so, perhaps the following exercise will help you identify your way of functioning at work.

Take a moment to think about your own life in order to determine how you may or may not be playing out your familial role in the workplace. Use the following exercise to identify and understand the role you played in your family and the role you have assumed at work. Once you do this, you can decide whether your behavior is helpful or detrimental to your ability to succeed in your job.

Role Identification Exercise

1. **What role did you occupy in your family?**_____

2. **Are you bringing your role into the workplace?**_____

3. **What behaviors do you exhibit at work that are similar to the ones you displayed within your family?**

    _____

4. **Do you believe that these behaviors are helping you to be successful in your job? If yes, how?**

    _____

5. **If no, how are your behaviors hindering you at work?**

    _____

•   •   •

Development of Childhood Roles

How do these roles develop? Children develop roles within the family through learned behaviors. They try something, it works, and they do it again. For example, take the little girl who overhears her parents arguing and goes in and tells them funny stories in order to distract them. If she is successful and they stop arguing, she has learned that she can make her parents stop fighting by entertaining them. This positive reinforcement encourages her to repeat the behavior, which is then incorporated into the way she sees herself. The little girl takes on the role of someone who keeps the peace by entertaining, and this role becomes part of her self-definition.

"I was told I was bright and extremely observant. Women in our family worked at interesting and challenging jobs, and they were valued and supported in the family. I came from a home where education was valued. I did well in school and was praised for my accomplishments. There was always talk in the house about school and grades and what the next goal and accomplishment would be." **Nancy—an Entrepreneur**

"In my generation, I was expected to marry and raise children. My dad was a difficult man to deal with. He was proud of the fact that I was smart and liked it when I entertained the family by singing. I was always trying to get his attention and appease him. My job was to please him." **Ilene—a Pleaser**

"Dad worked a lot of hours. It was Mom's job to take care of the house and all the kids, as well as work to help out with the bills. As kids, we were not encouraged to do much, as long as we did what was right and get it done. I was the quiet one, and I frequently felt intimidated by others in the family. Mom was always around, and I think you should always be around for your family." **Kate—a Survivor**

There are various other factors that contribute to the formation of roles, such as verbal messages and modeling. Verbal messages are statements made by family members that suggest a pattern of expectations and future behaviors. Messages such as "she's such a good girl" are both directional and reinforcing; they tell the child how to behave if she wants to maintain a favorable position within the family. The message is directional in that it directs a mode of behavior (i.e., do as you are told, follow instructions, follow the rules) and reinforcing in that it acknowledges the child for engaging in that behavior. Verbal messages are instrumental not only in the development of family roles but also in the formation of self-concept. We internalize these messages and incorporate them into our definitions of ourselves.

How We Learn Our Behaviors

"I was always a fiercely independent child, always my own person, and I was going to do what I wanted to do regardless of the consequences. My father wanted an all-American cheerleader daughter, and I was the antithesis. I wanted something different." **Jane—a Maverick**

Looking back, Jane, who occupied the role of the Maverick, recalls several messages that were contradictory, yet inadvertently pointed her in the direction of her future career.

Jane began to see herself as a Maverick because her beliefs and behaviors differed significantly from her parents' idea of what was appropriate for a girl. The messages she received were either criticisms or attempts to change her. She began to see her moves toward independence as acts of rebellion. Jane internalized this message and began to define herself as rebellious and difficult.

Many behaviors are learned through modeling, a process that teaches a pattern of behavior. In families, parents typically model behavior that is imitated by the children. Training a girl to be a woman begins at a very young age, when we start to assume the behaviors and language of our specific gender roles. As children engage in play, these roles are reinforced and provide the foundation for a larger set of "appropriate" or "right" behaviors. The payoff for appropriate behavior is acceptance, or fitting in, which enables us to maintain our relationship with others.

"The women in my family are artists. As a child, I talked about becoming an artist so that I would fit in with my mom and aunts. I believed that in order to be considered successful, I had to follow in the footsteps of the women in my family." **Lisa—a Peacekeeper**

As we grow, we become very conscious of how we are fitting in at home, with friends, and at school. Girls are supposed to act in a certain way, and if we do not, that makes us different and we are excluded. To be excluded is painful; it cuts to the quick of our very existence as women, the need to be connected and in relationship with others (Miller, 1991). Because of this need, we do whatever is necessary to fit in.

In their book *Meeting at the Crossroads* (1992), Lyn Mikel Brown and Carol Gilligan identify what adolescent girls do to fit in. They begin to modulate their voices and speak in ways that do not threaten relationships. They focus less on their own thoughts and desires and more on what others tell them they're supposed to think and want. Being one's own person is no longer a strength but a liability. They quiet their own voices and conform to cultural and societal standards in order to fit in.

The literature on human development states that men and women develop differently, which results in their different ways of functioning in the family and the workplace. According to this literature, little boys must separate from their mothers, due to the gender difference, in order to develop a masculine identity. This emphasis on separation as the necessary component for male development and self-definition is subsequently reinforced in the family and the workplace. From the time he is very young, a boy is told to "be a man," "stand up for yourself," and "fight your own battles." These phrases encourage him to take control and deal with things on his own. Throughout childhood and into adulthood, men are encouraged to acknowledge their strengths and power. This leads to positive beliefs about themselves, which translate into the ability to promote themselves and achieve success. For men, learning how to behave effectively in the workplace is a process that begins in childhood, continues into adulthood, and remains consistent within all contexts, including the family. In addition, men have developed and defined the rules of the workplace with an emphasis on separation and autonomy. Obeying these rules leads to success in the business world.

For women, the picture is quite different. Separation from the caregiver is not necessary for development to proceed. Typically, the caregiver is the same sex as the child, and the relationship remains intact and provides the blueprint for future relationships. Female children quickly learn to value relationships and engage in behaviors that are pleasing to others. The phrase "be a good little girl" suggests that compliance is a condition for maintaining connection. It encourages connection within relationships and contrasts markedly with the phrases encouraging autonomy that are told to little boys. In contrast to boys' acknowledgments of strength and power, girls learn that if they wish to remain connected to others, they must become as others see them, and in so doing, they are compelled to extinguish their individualism and autonomy. This process has led to identity confusion and subordination of self and has also inhibited women's professional growth within the male-defined and male-dominated workplace.

The family can be thought of as a system or organization, with each member of the organization assuming a different role. When we're growing up, we may learn our roles through the messages we receive from family members and from society at large; they teach or condition us to be who we are. We begin to be defined and identified by our behavior and our impact upon others. In return, the way others treat us and what they tell us about ourselves give us information about ourselves, and we use it to form our self-images. These messages play a critical part in our development by providing external validation for a particular mode of behavior when we are at our most impressionable stage of life. Stop and think about what messages you may have received from family members as you were growing up.

The "Should's" and the Workplace

In many ways, the messages we receive from our families are a method of transmitting the family rules. These are the family's beliefs and values, presented as "should's." In each family, there is a set of rules or "should's" that defines how each member should function. As women, each of us assumes a familial role because of these "should's." In some cases, we commit ourselves to the family norms and do whatever we think we must in order to maintain harmony and connection within our families. In other cases, we don't agree with the "should's" and are more concerned with maintaining a sense of individuality and pursuing our own vision, which can be interpreted as rebellious behavior. In either case, we carry the roles we assumed in childhood into our adult personal and professional relationships.

Like an individual or a family, an organization goes through a life cycle during which rules and "should's" are developed. These rules result from the way the leaders of a company translate their goals and vision into its formation and continuing evolution. Over the history of a company, a pattern of thinking, feeling, and functioning develops; this pattern has been identified as the company or organizational culture. We can think of the company culture and its procedures as the organization's rules or "should's." These rules are the messages that tell us how we should act, think, and speak if we want to be accepted within the company. They function much like the family rules or "should's." The purpose of both sets of messages is to mold us into the type of person who fits into the family or work environment. These rules then interact with each woman's conception of herself, which was formed through experiences she underwent before she entered the workplace. In examining how women play out their familial roles in the workplace, we will look at the interaction that takes place between those roles and the "should's" of the organization.

Conclusion

The interaction between their own views of themselves and the culture of their respective companies has led to mixed results for the six women we have been discussing. All of the women are very strong; however, some of them are more aware of their strengths than others.

Lisa, Jane, Rachel, and Jean have demonstrated tremendous strength within their roles. In her job search, each was very clear about the type of environment that would agree with her personality style.

Lisa chose to join a company whose culture fit her approach of creating teams in which the group members got along and worked well with one another. Creating a harmonious family structure has always been her primary goal, and this match between her personal aims and the culture of her employer has resulted in a very successful career for Lisa.

Jane, who has always had difficulty with authority figures and unquestioning obedience to rules, devoted her energies to finding a corporate culture that respected her individuality. After examining several opportunities, she joined a company where she was given enough autonomy not only to create her own work group but to design and implement its culture. This gave her control over her surroundings and allowed her to act independently, both of which have led to success.

Rachel is a take-charge type of person who needed to find a company that would respect her strength and offer an environment in which she could perform at optimum levels. She chose a job with a company that values strength and independent thinking. In her current position, she has the opportunity to direct a variety of projects, thus enabling her to apply her strong views to many aspects of the operation. The congruence between Rachel's values and the company culture has resulted in a win-win situation for everyone.

Jean has never allowed obstacles to prevent her from meeting her goals. When she realized that her medical condition was interfering with her ability to find a job, she decided to start her own company. In so doing, she created a company whose culture reflects her beliefs and values. Her prime objective has always been to help others, and in forming her own company, she has done just that. The company provides health care in a manner that respects the dignity of the individual. Each employee is schooled in that philosophy. Since Jean can no longer travel to the company's many branch offices, employees visit her on a regular basis to discuss business issues and the company's philosophy. Jean believes that her company's history and philosophy are what set it apart from others.

Ilene and Kate do not recognize their strengths as clearly as do Lisa, Jane, Rachel, and Jean. They were less sure about what type of work environment would be a good match for them. As a result, their work experiences have not been as rewarding and successful. They gravitated toward demanding, authoritarian employers with whom they replicate their family experiences. They did not do this intentionally; rather, they were drawn to a familiar personality style.

The stories of these six women illustrate how roles develop in the family and are then brought into the workplace. In some cases—such as with Lisa, Jane, Rachel, and Jean—the behaviors associated with those roles can lead to successful work experiences. For others, such as Ilene and Kate, continuing their family roles has confined them to frustration and lack of success at their jobs. In exploring women's behavior in the workplace as a function of their development, we have theorized that the roles women assumed in their families of origin formed the basis for their adult personal and professional roles. In other words, the information women receive about themselves from others contributes to the self-images they form as children and young adults and lays the groundwork for their adult styles of behavior. In the following chapters, we will discuss each of the six roles in greater detail.

"As a child, my role was to keep everything functioning smoothly, and it continues into my adult life. I am the stabilizing force in my family and at work."

2   ROLE OF THE PEACEKEEPER

These are the words Lisa used to describe her role as a child in her family and as an adult. For Lisa and others who act as Peacekeepers, the goal is to avoid conflict and maintain emotional connection with the people in their lives. The behaviors associated with this role illustrate the importance of connection in women's lives.

The Peacekeeper can be characterized as someone who works to maintain harmonious environments in all areas of her life. She distracts others with her entertaining behavior and by defusing conflict before it begins. The Peacekeeper refrains from expressing her own thoughts and opinions because they might be incompatible with the thoughts and opinions of others and could eventually lead to problems. Her use of distraction and repression is a direct attempt to avoid conflict. There is a reciprocal interaction between the behavior the Peacekeeper exhibits, the reaction it elicits, and her subsequent behaviors. This interaction forms the foundation for the way she functions in the workplace.

Workplace Behaviors

In the office, the Peacekeeper's early training in conflict avoidance is apparent in the way she interacts with difficult people and diverse groups of coworkers. She listens and observes, then strives to build bridges and create unanimity among them. Her greatest strengths are her team-building and leadership capabilities. Her sensitivity to the feelings of others enables her to diplomatically integrate the thoughts and opinions of all parties involved. In her efforts to preserve harmony, the Peacekeeper is hypervigilant in identifying potential or emerging conflict. She immediately attempts either to refocus attention away from the source of the problem or to mediate some kind of speedy consensus.

There are both positive and negative aspects associated with the role of Peacekeeper at work. The positive aspects include increased awareness of the environment and, specifically, heightened sensitivity to the emotional needs of those around her. The Peacekeeper relates easily to all types of individuals and demonstrates her confidence in her ability by engaging in banter and other lighthearted forms of interaction. She reads her work environment and her coworkers very well and adapts readily to both of them. These attributes are an advantage when navigating the political waters that exist in every organization, regardless of size or type of industry. The Peacekeeper knows how to operate in a system.

A negative aspect of the Peacekeeper role is her lack of individual professional development as she devotes all of her energies to avoiding conflict. Because of her single-minded efforts, the Peacekeeper may not develop the conflict-management skills that are essential for any leadership position. Concentrating solely on avoiding conflict leads to a tendency to focus excessively on others. Often, the Peacekeeper will deny her own perspective in favor of the company's view, thereby maintaining peace at work.

THE PEACEKEEPER: CHARACTER SUMMARY

Strengths	Weaknesses
Sensitive to others	Extremely sensitive to the environment
Good listening skills	Poor conflict-management skills
Aware of environment	Avoids taking risks
Able to defuse potentially problematic situations	Hesitates to speak up for herself
Adapts to various environments	Lack of individuality
Team builder	Repressed creativity
Politically savvy	

Peacekeeper Self-Evaluation

Now that you have read over the general characteristics, both positive and negative, of the Peacekeeper role, can you identify with this role?

_____

If so, what behaviors of the Peacekeeper role do you engage in?

_____

Have the behaviors of the Peacekeeper role enhanced your success? If so, how?

_____

_____

Have the behaviors of the Peacekeeper role hindered your success? If so, how?

_____

_____

● ● · ●

While this behavior maintains a peaceful environment, it also impedes the development of individuality on the part of the Peacekeeper and consequently sabotages her success at work. She typically is not a renegade, visionary, or entrepreneur because she is too heavily focused on and invested in the culture and current procedures of the organization. Working within the culture is important; however, success demands the willingness to take risks from time to time. The Peacekeeper weighs each new idea carefully before suggesting it to her senior management. She hesitates to introduce innovations because she thinks primarily of the risks involved in altering the status quo. The Peacekeeper fears potential failure and falling out of favor with those who occupy positions of power. The behaviors of the Peacekeeper often sabotage her professional success.

The Peacekeeper is extremely sensitive to her environment. It is helpful to visualize the Peacekeeper's sensitivity to the environment on a scale. Sensitivity to the environment includes sensitivity to others, such as boss, coworkers, and staff; sensitivity to company culture; and sensitivity to self. In discussing the positive and negative aspects of the Peacekeeper role, we have indicated that the behaviors we employ to avoid conflict can be a double-edged sword. In other words, one's sensitivity to others can be both positive and negative with regard to success in the workplace. It is our belief that it is the extent of the Peacekeeper's conflict avoidance behavior, not the behavior itself, that determines whether the consequence is negative, and hinders success, or positive, and facilitates success.

If you can identify with the role of the Peacekeeper, take a moment to rate your sensitivity to others, company culture, and self on the following scales. You can then determine for yourself how helpful your sensitivity and behaviors are to your career.

Sensitivity to Environment Exercise

0% = Least sensitivity   100% = Greatest sensitivity

1. People: Sensitivity to Others

0%	10	20	30	40	50	60	70	80	90	100%

2. Culture: Sensitivity to Company Culture

0%	10	20	30	40	50	60	70	80	90	100%

3. Self: Sensitivity to Self

0%	10	20	30	40	50	60	70	80	90	100%

•   •   •

If an individual shows no sensitivity to the needs of coworkers, she would be at the 0% end of the Sensitivity to Others scale and would be experiencing constant difficulties at work. This type of behavior would almost certainly sabotage her chances for professional success. Likewise, if she disregards the culture of the company and persistently opposes its usual procedures, she would be at 0% on the Sensitivity to Company Culture scale and would again be sabotaging her ability to succeed at work. Because of her exclusive focus on avoiding conflict, the Peacekeeper usually falls somewhere in the 80% to 100% range on these two scales. At the same time, the Peacekeeper typically falls in the 0% to 20% range on the Sensitivity to Self scale, due to her tendency to repress her own ideas in the interests of maintaining harmonious relationships with her coworkers.

A more balanced perspective on the three environmental elements—others, company culture, and self—will allow the Peacekeeper to acknowledge her own needs for growth while integrating these needs with those of the organization. This balance of others, culture, and self will lead to greater success for all concerned. The goal is to register between 50% and 60% on each scale, which represents a healthier alternative to the Peacekeeper's hypersensitivity to others. In turn, this more balanced behavior will lead to individual development and success in the workplace.

Two Styles of the Peacekeeper Role

There are many different ways of functioning within the Peacekeeper role. These behaviors vary depending on the personality of the individual. We will now take a more detailed look at how the Peacekeeper role develops and plays out in the cases of two women, Lisa and Joan.

Lisa is a thirty-nine-year-old human resources executive who works for a large, professional services firm. She is a friendly, confident, and outgoing woman who avoids conflict by utilizing her team-building skills and creating consensus in her work environment.

"My primary focus has been on getting people to interact as a team. I need to get them to think like a team and function as a group to enhance their success. They need to lean on one another. I'm used to a team environment with group dynamics and communication, and I instinctively work that way. When a decision is being made, I know who needs to buy into that decision before it can be a real decision. I am able to get people to buy in and develop consensus because I have gained the trust of my colleagues." **Lisa—a Peacekeeper**

The following vignette illustrates Lisa's consensus-building behavior. During weekly staff meetings, Lisa deliberately refrains from voicing her thoughts and opinions in order to give her coworkers the chance to develop their own acceptance for the ideas under discussion and reach an agreement on how to proceed. She believes it is her job as a leader to empower her coworkers and develop future leaders by first teaching them the importance of building team consensus.

Lisa is a democratic leader and, despite her position of authority, always seeks consensus. She is fair, participative, and has very strong team-building skills. Lisa strives to maintain peace in her work environment by trying to satisfy everyone who is involved in a project. She is a dynamic, unselfish worker and leader who acts as an advocate for the people in her group and utilizes her strong verbal communication skills to maintain a conflict-free community.

Lisa thinks her ability to get staff members in her department to commit themselves to a project and work together as a team is a positive component of her Peacekeeper role. Her skill in building relationships that contribute to her success is evident in her interactions with her superiors and with those who work for her. Respect and belief in her capabilities mark the relationships she maintains with the partners of her firm. Respect and her belief in their ability to manage their respective functions also mark her relationships with the people she manages. Within her position, she enjoys a great deal of freedom and control.

Lisa has worked hard, paid her dues, and risen to some extent within the corporate structure. She is very politically aware and sociable. She is particularly adept at reading a situation and acting accordingly. She exudes confidence, and others enjoy being around her—everybody likes her. Lisa takes pride in creating a family in every work group, whether she is a participant or a leader. She is a relationship builder with very strong interpersonal skills. Her ability to observe and understand her environment has helped her succeed.

"I feel like I have a lot of control, but it also may be that I understand what's meant by control. My understanding of control isn't absolute power to micro-manage the people who work with me. I have no interest in that. I want them to be the experts."
Lisa—a Peacekeeper

Lisa chose to join a company whose culture fit her approach of creating teams in which the members all get along and work well with one another. Creating a harmonious family structure has always been Lisa's goal. The agreement between her personal goals and the culture of her employer has contributed to her professional success.

Negative aspects of her role include her tendency to stifle her creativity in order to support the company culture and her exclusive focus on others. Because of these negatives, she has been unable to meet her own professional needs, and her limited advancement in the company has in turn led to frustration. At work, she maintains her role as the Peacekeeper by being a problem solver and troubleshooter. Lisa remains the consummate Peacekeeper.

"I've watched the people who advance in my company, and I've observed what they do in order to advance. People advance because they get consensus from coworkers before they take a step, unlike those people who just plow ahead and ultimately plow into a wall." **Lisa—a Peacekeeper**

Joan, a thirty-year-old woman who works for a large financial services company, represents a different version of the Peacekeeper. She is timid and quiet and avoids conflict by refusing to speak up or question authority. This behavior developed as a result of the messages she received as a child.

Some Peacekeepers avoid conflict and maintain harmonious relationships by silencing themselves. They refrain from expressing their thoughts and opinions in

> "Authority figures are right, adults are right, you don't question them, you don't talk back to them, you respect them. My sister and I were taught not to stand up for ourselves, but rather to just be there and obey and everything would be fine. When I'm at work, I keep my thoughts and opinions to myself in an effort to maintain peaceful relationships with my coworkers. I'm hesitant to tell people they are doing something incorrectly or to point out a better way of handling a situation for fear of creating tension. I believe that functioning as a manager would create tension between my coworkers and myself, so I have chosen not to seek or accept a managerial position."
>
> **Joan—a Peacekeeper**

order to avoid any possible disagreement that may result from what they say. Joan's hesitancy to speak up is exhibited at work in her reluctance to seek or accept a managerial position. She believes that being in a position of authority would create conflict and tension in her work environment.

The obvious negative consequence of this behavior is failure to advance. The positive aspect of her behavior is the good working relationships she enjoys with her coworkers. Balance once again becomes the issue. If she were able to balance her concern for others with confidence in her ability to manage them in a respectful manner, she might be able to take the risk of moving up in her company. The key is in looking at alternatives to her initial idea that accepting a managerial position would create conflict and tension in her relationships with her coworkers.

The Relationship Between Self-Concept and Behavior

These brief discussions of Lisa and Joan describe two styles of the Peacekeeper role. Lisa tries to maintain a harmonious environment by always seeking consensus among her coworkers. Joan avoids conflict by denying herself opportunities for advancement. For both Lisa and Joan, their conceptions of themselves and their abilities had a significant impact on their behaviors. In order to create a more integrated and balanced approach to their work, they first have to become aware of the thoughts that preserve their current modes of behavior.

The following Work Role Exercise is a tool to help you change the way you tend to act as a Peacekeeper. The purpose of this exercise is threefold: (1) to identify the thoughts that maintain your role; (2) to change your thinking, which will then change your behavior; and (3) to create a plan for changing your behavior.

Peacekeeper Work Role Exercise

1. **What thoughts do you have about yourself that maintain the role of Peacekeeper?**

    _____

    _____

2. **What evidence supports these thoughts?**

    _____

    _____

3. **What evidence disputes these thoughts?**

    _____

    _____

4. **What alternative behavior(s) would you like to exhibit?**

    _____

    _____

5. **What steps must you take in the short term (3–6 months) to progress toward this new behavior?**

    Step 1_____

    Step 2_____

    Step 3_____

6. **What steps must you take in the long term (1–3 years) to progress toward this new behavior?**

    Step 1_____

    Step 2_____

    Step 3_____

7. What thoughts may interfere with your taking these steps?

_____

_____

8. What would you tell a friend who shared these concerns with you? Write down this alternative perspective and use it to motivate yourself to start changing your behavior.

_____

_____

•   •   •

Conclusion

Women develop through connection with the people in their lives. The Peace-keeper role illustrates how some women maintain these connections. A Peacekeeper learns her role early in life, within her family. As she grows, she develops behaviors designed to maintain a harmonious home environment. She practices these behaviors over the years until the role becomes automatic at home and at work.

While you may not be able to pinpoint exactly what you are doing, you do know how you feel. The next time you are unhappy at work, stop and think about your behaviors and how they may be hindering or facilitating your success. If you recognize elements of yourself in the Peacekeeper role, you can implement change by using the exercises in this chapter and by identifying the behaviors you would like to stop, start, and continue.

THE PEACEKEEPER: A PLAN OF ACTION

Stop	Avoiding risks
	Holding back your thoughts
	Focusing completely on others
Start	Expressing your thoughts and opinions
	Dealing with conflict
	Focusing on your own needs
	Being more sensitive to yourself
Continue	Being sensitive to others
	Being a team builder
	Being a good listener
	Being politically savvy

The Peacekeeper may find herself trapped in a low-level, dead-end position if she represses her own views and continues to concentrate on avoiding conflict. However, her strengths exemplify her excellent interpersonal skills. Given her ability to create good working relationships, opportunities for advancement in the company are limitless. It is necessary for the Peacekeeper to put more emphasis on her strengths and create a balanced and integrated approach in order to develop a winning role.

"Ever since I was a kid, I always thought I knew the right way to do something. I need to have things my way, and that creates some difficulties at work. It's either going to be on my terms or not at all."

3 ROLE OF THE MAVERICK

Jane used these words to describe herself as a child in her family and as an adult. For Jane and others who occupy the Maverick role, the goal is to live life on their own terms, to maintain their independence despite societal pressures to conform. This role typically results when definitive expectations established by the family and peer group are not consistent with the individual's personality. A child with a weak sense of self may acquiesce and become a Pleaser, but one with a strong sense of self will buck the trend and follow her own sense of what is right for her. This is the path chosen by Jane and Mary, the two women we will discuss in this chapter.

The Maverick can be characterized as someone who is fiercely independent and willing to deal with the consequences of charting her own unique course through life. This perspective certainly has its challenges; however, it allows the individual to be true to herself. At work, the Maverick will often appear inflexible, rigid, and insular, yet strong and competent at the same time. People who do not work with her directly think it would be difficult to associate with her. However, those who do work with her place a high value on her intelligence and competence and the community she creates within her group.

Workplace Behaviors

To accomplish the tasks before her, the Maverick creates a cohesive and loyal work group with its own culture. This group generally adopts her perspective on how things should be done. She usually does not become involved in organizational politics but instead follows her intuition about what it takes to be successful. While she is aware of company culture and politics, she does not feel obligated to accept their dictates, and if they do not fit in with what she perceives as the requirements for her success, she will disregard them. The Maverick is a complex individual, with the capacity to be a break-out success or an organizational outcast. Her level of success is determined by the company's flexibility and acceptance of her type of personality.

There are positive and negative aspects associated with the role of the Maverick at work. The positive aspects include her intelligence, her strong belief in her convictions, and her sense of independence and individuality. The Maverick is blessed with the kind of self-awareness and self-confidence that enable her to stand apart from the crowd and dare to take risks. She typically is a creative problem solver and an industrious worker. Although she may appear aloof, when she finds people who respect her style and whom she respects, she is an excellent leader. She cares a great deal about the people with whom she works closely.

The negative aspects of the role include inflexibility, difficulty in adapting to environments that do not support her independent style, and minimal tolerance for those who disagree with her. Her singular focus often blinds her to viable alternatives that may be suggested by others. The Maverick is selective about her coworkers. When compelled to work with those who do not share her perspective or whom she does not respect, she can be impatient and is often thought of as difficult. Given her need to follow her own path, the Maverick usually has a hard time with authority figures. These traits often end up isolating the Maverick within the organization and can affect her opportunities for advancement in an extremely negative way.

THE MAVERICK: CHARACTER SUMMARY

Strengths	Weaknesses
Independent	Inflexible
Self-assured	Difficulty working with others
Takes risks	Impatient
Develops positive relationships	Not a team player
Creative	Difficulty adapting to new environments
Problem solver	Difficulty with authority figures
Works hard	Not open to alternative opinions

Maverick Self-Evaluation

Now that you have read over the general characteristics, both positive and negative, of the Maverick, can you identify with this role?

_____

If so, what behaviors of the Maverick role do you engage in?

_____

Have the behaviors of the Maverick role enhanced your success? If so, how?

_____

_____

Have the behaviors of the Maverick role hindered your success? If so, how?

_____

_____

• • •

In terms of sensitivity to the work environment, the Maverick presents a varied and interesting picture. While she may at times appear to be an unconcerned, independent individual within the company at large, she is very committed to those with whom she works closely. It is helpful to visualize the Maverick's behavior on a scale. Sensitivity to the environment includes sensitivity to others, such as boss, coworkers, and staff; sensitivity to company culture; and sensitivity to self. It is important to note that being sensitive to coworkers contributes to more positive work relationships and displaying insensitive behavior results in difficult work relationships.

The following scales are designed to help you determine your degree of sensitivity to the various elements in the workplace and whether your behavior produces negative consequences that hinder your success or positive ones that facilitate your success. If you can identify with the role of the Maverick, take a moment to rate your sensitivity to others, company culture, and self on the following scales. You can then determine for yourself how beneficial your sensitivity and behaviors are to your career.

Sensitivity to Environment Exercise

0% = Least sensitivity   100% = Greatest sensitivity

1. People: Sensitivity to Others

0%	10	20	30	40	50	60	70	80	90	100%

2. Culture: Sensitivity to Company Culture

0%	10	20	30	40	50	60	70	80	90	100%

3. Self: Sensitivity to Self

0%	10	20	30	40	50	60	70	80	90	100%

• • •

If an individual shows no sensitivity to the needs of coworkers, she would be at the 0% end of the Sensitivity to Others scale and would constantly be experiencing difficulties at work. This type of behavior would almost certainly sabotage her chances for success. Likewise, if she disregards the culture of the company and persistently opposes its standard procedures, she would be at the 0% end of the Sensitivity to Company Culture scale and would again be sabotaging her chances for success. The Maverick usually falls somewhere in the 50% to 60% range on the first of these two scales because she exhibits some sensitivity to those with whom she works very closely. When it comes to the people in her work group, especially those who share her perspective, she would fall in the 80% to 100% range. However, her sensitivity level decreases significantly for authority figures and those who are outside her small group or who do not share her vision of the way the work should be done. With them, she registers in the 0% to 20% range. Averaging these two brings her into the 50% to 60% range on the Sensitivity to Others scale. The Maverick usually falls somewhere in the 0% to 20% range on the Sensitivity to Company Culture scale. Given her minimal regard for corporate culture, she often experiences difficulties at work, such as the inability to secure approval or funding for new projects or the hiring of additional staff. Her lack of sensitivity to company culture sabotages her ability to be successful at work.

On the other hand, due to her independence and self-assurance about her professional abilities, the Maverick typically falls in the 80% to 100% range on the Sensitivity to Self scale. She is sensitive to her needs in that she chooses her own way of working and with whom she will work. She believes she knows what is right for her; this contributes to her position on the Sensitivity to Self scale.

Identifying your range of behaviors on the above scales will heighten your awareness of how you function within your work environment. You can then decide whether your behaviors are helpful, and facilitate your success, or detrimental, and hinder your success. The Maverick must take the time to understand whose opinions and decisions are important and why she must enlist their support, which means being more sensitive to those in leadership positions. In joining an organization, she made a decision to become a part of it. Working in isolation may at times be at cross-purposes with her ability to succeed within the organization. Applying a more balanced perspective to the three elements related to sensitivity to the environment would allow the Maverick to acknowledge and integrate her own needs for growth with the needs of the organization. This balance of people, culture, and self will lead to greater success for all concerned.

Two Styles of the Maverick Role

"I grew up in an environment where I had to struggle to some extent for attention. I have experienced this in my professional life as well. I often wonder whether I am just reliving my past experiences or if these situations are really happening. Ever since I was a kid, I always thought I knew the right way to do something. I'm very impatient with the way things are, and I need to have things my way, and that creates some difficulties at work."

Jane—a Maverick

As with all of these roles, there are different ways of being a Maverick, depending on the personality of the individual. We will now take a more detailed look at how the Maverick role developed and is played out for two women, Jane and Mary.

Jane is a fifty-five-year-old partner in a large international consulting firm. She grew up in a middle-class family with her mother, father, and younger sister. She was a very strong and independent child who struggled to find a way to fit in at home and at school. Her parents' expectations were inconsistent with her own self-image and expectations. This caused her parents to label her as rebellious. Jane did not think of her behavior as rebellious but as an attempt to maintain independence. Issues of independence and control were important in Jane's childhood and have carried over into her professional life.

"I push things they don't necessarily want pushed. I aggravate a lot of people because I won't accept the rules if, in my view, the rules are not compatible with what I'm trying to achieve." **Jane—a Maverick**

Jane is fortunate because she is in a position to create and lead her own work group within the larger company. She developed this group according to her vision of how things should be and hired people who share her vision. In this way, she controls the culture of her daily work environment. She acknowledges that she is most comfortable with her group because they mirror her style of working.

The following vignette illustrates her thinking regarding her role as a group leader and the opportunity to control her own environment. When Jane's company was considering a merger with another company, her employees asked her if she was going to leave if she couldn't maintain her leadership position in the group. She replied that she did not care if she led the group or not; what mattered to her was being able to do what she wanted to do, in the way she wanted to do it. Jane cares a great deal about having the flexibility to function as she wishes at work.

Jane has a difficult time with authority figures. She attributes this to the relationship she had with her father, who set himself up as an authority figure who could not be questioned. As a result, she is unable to accept authority figures whom she cannot question.

In her professional life, she has sought to maintain freedom and independence in order to follow the path she believes is right for her and for the clients she serves. Despite the difficulties of some of her interpersonal relationships, Jane has been extremely successful in her professional life.

> "I have a lot of trouble with people who are authority figures just because they are in a particular position. I have no respect for them. By and large, I am not very good with authority figures. But I am better at dealing with authority figures whom I respect."
>
> **Jane—a Maverick**

Jane is highly respected and well regarded. Yet she is misunderstood, much as she was when she was young. As a child, she was rebellious, unwilling to go with the flow. As a professional, she is rebellious and wants things done her way. Typically she builds strong relationships with those over whom she has direct control. But within the larger organization, she is seen as difficult to work with and a threat to the status quo.

Mary is a forty-two-year-old director of admissions for a small liberal arts college. She is one of five children and grew up in a large working-class family. Her parents' goal for their children was that they graduate high school and find a good job with good benefits. Mary did not share her parents' perspective; she had different aspirations for herself, to go to college and become a teacher. This made her an outcast within her own family. Despite their negative comments and general lack of support, Mary pursued her dream and found a way to accomplish her goal. She brings this same focus and determination to her work.

> "I feel as though I'm always struggling to get my point across regardless of the issue under discussion. My coworkers and I seem to have a different perspective on how things should be handled. I would like to spend less energy defending my perspective and more energy executing my ideas."
>
> **Mary—a Maverick**

A very intelligent woman, Mary has strong opinions about the way things should be handled. She runs her department in an extremely orderly, structured manner that reflects her views on proper procedure. She presents herself as the unequivocal director of her department and has little or no tolerance for dissenting opinions. She is frequently in conflict with her colleagues over matters of college policy.

Mary has intense feelings about the need to maintain her position on issues; at times, this inflexibility results in her feeling like an outcast at work. Her unwillingness to temper her unique perspective inhibits her ability to build good working relationships with her colleagues.

Having the courage to pursue what you believe is right for you regardless of the obstacles is a trait to be admired and valued. The difficulty often experienced by Mavericks in the workplace is being able to recognize when their tenacity is not working. That is when the Maverick must step back and reassess the situation to determine a more effective way of getting what she wants. The ability to do this often makes the difference between the Maverick's professional success or failure. This concept is exemplified in the experiences of Jane and Mary. The difference between Jane and Mary with regard to their Maverick role is that Jane is more adept at working within a system. Although Jane is often inflexible in her perceptions, she realizes that there can be more than one path to attaining her goal. When she sees that she is fighting a losing battle, she reassesses the situation and develops a new approach. She focuses mainly on reaching her goal, not on how she's going to get there. In addition to her adaptability, Jane has also found a system that is more amenable to her Maverick work style. Mary, on the other hand, is continuously fighting an uphill battle. Her inability to recognize when she must step back and reassess a situation often leads to conflict with her colleagues and frustration on her part. She is not as proficient at working within a system; her current work environment would function more smoothly with a more compliant individual.

The Relationship Between Self-Concept and Behavior

In the cases of both Jane and Mary, the behaviors they exhibit in the workplace are a function of their earlier life experiences and the thoughts they had about themselves as children, which they still carry with them as adults. In order to create a more balanced approach in their work styles, they first had to become aware of the thoughts that maintain their current behaviors.

The following Work Role Exercise is one method of becoming more aware of your thoughts. The purpose of this exercise is threefold: (1) to identify the thoughts that maintain your role; (2) to change your thinking, which will then change your behavior; and (3) to create a plan for changing your behavior.

Maverick Work Role Exercise

1. **What thoughts do you have about yourself that maintain the role of the Maverick?**

   _____

   _____

2. **What evidence supports these thoughts?**

   _____

   _____

3. **What evidence disputes these thoughts?**

   _____

   _____

4. **What alternative behavior(s) would you like to exhibit?**

   _____

   _____

5. **What steps must you take in the short term (3–6 months) to progress toward this new behavior?**

   Step 1_____

   Step 2_____

   Step 3_____

6. **What steps must you take in the long term (1–3 years) to progress toward this new behavior?**

   Step 1_____

   Step 2_____

   Step 3_____

7. What thoughts may interfere with your taking these steps?

_____

_____

8. What would you tell a friend who shared these concerns with you? Write down this alternative perspective and use it to motivate yourself to start changing your behavior.

_____

_____

● ● ●

Conclusion

One of the major traps for the Maverick is being boxed in by her own inflexibility. She may be so focused on one issue that she fails to see the bigger picture. She takes a microview of situations. The Maverick also restricts herself by her reluctance to build relationships with people outside her area of expertise and her refusal to use her expertise as leverage with others. This may lead to lost business opportunities and missed chances for greater success.

Working with a Maverick can be both exhilarating and frustrating. She can be innovative in her vision for various projects. She can also be frustrating because of her inability to work within the system to bring her projects to fruition. Her working style can make life difficult for those who work closely with her. She places them in the position of having to declare their loyalties. If her coworkers do not consistently agree with her perspective, she separates herself from them. Yet if they do not remain loyal to the company culture, they will become outcasts within the organization.

The Maverick would benefit greatly from learning to create balance between her needs and the needs of her coworkers. But in order to change our behavior, we must first become aware of it. Most of the time, our behavior is so automatic that we are not even aware of what we are doing. You can implement change by using the exercises in this chapter and by identifying the behaviors you would like to stop, start, and continue.

THE MAVERICK: A PLAN OF ACTION

Stop	Being inflexible
	Closing yourself off to the ideas of others
	Alienating yourself from the system
Start	Building relationships with colleagues both in and out of your department
	Being more sensitive to the politics and culture of the organization
	Working within the system to create change
Continue	Building community and strong relationships within your own department
	Being innovative in your approach to work
	Maintaining your spirit and individuality

The role of the Maverick is associated with many strengths and positive behaviors. Her innovativeness, creativity, and ability to think strategically are attributes to be admired and emulated by others. Developing positive working relationships with colleagues as well as becoming more sensitive to company culture will enable the Maverick to achieve greater success and a winning role.

"As a child, as long as I did what everyone else wanted me to do, they liked me. Somehow I got the message that good girls do what they are told and follow the rules. This message stayed with me, and as a working adult, I believe that I allowed myself to be taken advantage of in order to gain the admiration of my superiors."

4 ROLE OF THE PLEASER

These are the words Ilene used to describe her role as a child in her family and as an adult. For Ilene and others who occupy the Pleaser role, the goal is to be accepted and liked. The role typically develops out of the modeling the child observes in the household as one parent subordinates her needs to the other parent in order to be accepted and valued. The child quickly learns and implements this behavior. The Pleaser behavior is then reinforced by the positive attention the child receives when she is rewarded with praise and approval.

The Pleaser can be characterized as respectful, obedient, and cooperative. She is usually so anxious to please everyone in her family and work environment that she neither develops nor expresses any of her own thoughts and opinions. The Pleaser tries to satisfy everyone in hopes that people will think well of her and like her. She will often say things to people that she believes they want to hear even if she doesn't have the authority or the ability to follow through on what she has said. While she is attempting to avoid conflict, her prime concern is internal; thus her low self-esteem, which is due in large part to the belief that she is not good enough. To compensate for this belief, she will frequently try to emulate the behavior of other people as a way of gaining acceptance. She believes she has value as an individual only when she is receiving validation from others. In an effort to obtain this validation, she subordinates her own identity. As she tries to be everything to everyone, she pays a great price, for she never has the opportunity to develop her own identity.

Workplace Behaviors

In the workplace, the Pleaser will accept whatever task is given to her regardless of how she feels about it or whether it even falls within her job description. Her coworkers and superiors are often able to take advantage of her because she is reluctant to say "no" or even speak her own mind.

There are both positive and negative aspects associated with the role of the Pleaser at work. Positive aspects include her ability to get along with people and develop agreeable relationships. Her good listening skills, readiness to ask questions, and ability to concentrate fully on what the other person has to say enable the Pleaser to understand and respond in a way that satisfies others. She adapts well to a variety of environments by ingratiating herself and creating the reputation of being available for others. Her desire to please and receive praise in return makes her a good worker who can concentrate on a task and get it done in a timely manner. She follows through on all of her commitments and consequently is often in demand for a variety of projects. Cooperation, diligence, and a sense of responsibility mark her working style. This easygoing employee takes direction without question.

THE PLEASER: CHARACTER SUMMARY

Strengths	Weaknesses
Gets along well with others	Avoids taking risks
Listens well	Denies own needs
Adapts to various environments	Lacks individuality
Develops positive relationships	Overextends self
Cooperative	Unable to set limits
Hardworking	Insecure
Sensitive to the needs of others	Easily taken advantage of

Pleaser Self-Evaluation

Now that you have read over the general characteristics, both positive and negative, of the Pleaser, can you identify with this role?

_____

If so, what behaviors of the Pleaser role do you engage in?

_____

Have the behaviors of the Pleaser role enhanced your success? If so, how?

_____

_____

Have the behaviors of the Pleaser role hindered your success? If so, how?

_____

_____

• • •

Negative aspects of the role include her reluctance to take risks or commit herself to an opinion regarding any issue. Her need for approval is so great that she frequently puts her own professional life on hold to please others. The Pleaser becomes so adept at doing what others want and saying what she believes others want to hear that she never develops her own perspective. This lack of individuality is detrimental to the Pleaser's professional advancement, for although she works well with others, she probably is not seen as a creative problem solver in her own right. She tends to get involved in too many projects, thus stretching her capacities to the limit. Sometimes she takes on more than she can handle, and this leads to problems with coworkers. Her difficulty in saying "no" and setting limits on her responsibilities often leads to a great deal of stress. When faced with conflict or disagreement, the Pleaser seeks to appease rather than risk alienation from anyone. This method of resolving conflict is often seen as weak and contributes significantly to missed opportunities for promotion to upper management positions.

The Pleaser's feelings of insecurity, which result from her inability to generate her own sense of validation, contribute to her high degree of sensitivity to the environment. By pleasing others, she obtains their approval. This external validation provides her with the sense of worth that she cannot obtain for herself. Given the important role that the environment plays in her feelings of self-worth, it is understandable that her sensitivity to the environment should be high. Sensitivity to the environment includes sensitivity to others, such as boss, coworkers, and staff; sensitivity to company culture; and sensitivity to self. The following scales are designed to help you understand that it is not necessarily the behavior itself that is good or bad; rather, it is the degree to which one engages in the identified behavior that determines whether the consequence is negative, and hinders success, or positive, and facilitates success.

If you can identify with the role of the Pleaser, then take a moment to rate your sensitivity to others, company culture, and self on the following scales. You can then determine for yourself how helpful your sensitivity and behaviors are to your career.

Sensitivity to Environment Exercise

0% = Least sensitivity   100% = Greatest sensitivity

1. People: Sensitivity to Others

0%	10	20	30	40	50	60	70	80	90	100%

2. Culture: Sensitivity to Company Culture

0%	10	20	30	40	50	60	70	80	90	100%

3. Self: Sensitivity to Self

0%	10	20	30	40	50	60	70	80	90	100%

•   •   •

If a person shows no sensitivity to the needs of coworkers, she would be at the 0% end of the Sensitivity to Others scale and would be experiencing continuous difficulties at work. This type of behavior would almost certainly sabotage her chances for professional success. Likewise, if she disregards the culture of the company and persistently opposes its usual procedures, she would be at the 0% end of the Sensitivity to Company Culture scale and would again be hampering her own success. The Pleaser, like the Caregiver and the Peacekeeper, usually falls somewhere in the 80% to 100% range on the Sensitivity to Others and Sensitivity to Company Culture scales. The 80% to 100% range indicates a disproportionate focus on pleasing others and complying with company culture, and in doing so, the Pleaser ignores her own needs and perspectives at work. She totally disregards herself in order to ingratiate herself with coworkers so she will be liked and valued. As a result of this focus on others, the Pleaser typically falls in the 0% to 20% range on the Sensitivity to Self scale. As we have stated previously, the Pleaser must seek external validation to compensate for what she cannot give herself, an internal sense of self-worth.

Identifying where your behaviors fall on these scales will heighten your awareness of how you function at work. With this awareness, you can identify whether your behaviors are valued by your organization and are putting you on the right path for success or if your company is taking advantage of you and passing you over for promotions. While it may seem that any company would value a person who seeks to please and appease her coworkers, this may not be the case. The Pleaser may find her opportunities for advancement are limited in a company that respects and values individuality and risk taking as opposed to her type of ingratiating behavior. However, a company that prefers employees who commit themselves to the company culture with no questions asked, rather than employees who risk introducing new concepts, may reward the Pleaser for her behavior.

The Pleaser must take the time to identify what her behaviors are and how they fit into the culture of the company. If, after completing the exercise, you realize that your focus is skewed in the direction of others, you have the opportunity to begin creating a more equitable perspective. A balance of others, culture, and self will lead to greater success for all concerned. You as an individual will attain a stronger sense of who you are and what you think. You will then be able to develop meaningful relationships with your coworkers. Finally, your company will be better served by a thinking, contributing individual than by a yes-person. Strive for 50% to 60% on each of the three scales. This level of integration will lead to more balanced behaviors and is a healthier alternative to the Pleaser's need to win external validation by subordinating her needs to the needs of others. This in turn will result in individual development and success in the workplace.

Two Styles of the Pleaser Role

Most of us have come across Pleasers in our offices; we may know them by other names, but their behaviors are similar. In the following paragraphs, we will introduce you to Ilene and Sarah, two women who we believe characterize the Pleaser role.

Ilene is a forty-four-year-old assistant vice president in a financial services company. She has spent her entire life trying to please others by doing what everyone else tells her she should do. She is very adept at taking directions without asking questions and does whatever is required to be accepted and become an integral part of the unit to which she is assigned.

An example of Ilene's workplace behavior is illustrated in the following vignette. Ilene was upset about the new project to which she had been assigned. She had little experience with the type of work and was uncomfortable with the other people in the work group. Despite these concerns, she agreed to accept the project so she wouldn't displease her boss. Ilene's prime concern was that her boss and the powers-that-be like her and do not see her as a problem.

Whenever Ilene is asked to take on additional responsibilities at her firm, her response is always "I'll be happy to, thank you for thinking of me." While others may balk at constantly being given more work, Ilene sees these requests as validation, which helps her feel better about herself.

Her Pleaser behavior works well for her because it matches up with the culture of the company. She does not try to fight or change the culture; she fits right into it. She grew up with this culture and understands it well. It requires unquestioning adherence to the dictates of upper management. In addition, another clearly communicated message is that employees should feel honored to be part of the company and should demonstrate their gratitude by agreeing to do whatever is asked of them. In short, the company is run like a family dominated by a strong, male authority figure. This is a familiar and comfortable environment for Ilene, since she grew up in a family that was run by her authoritarian father.

> "When I first started working for this company, I wanted desperately to be noticed and liked by my new boss. In order to accomplish this, I agreed to do all that was asked of me; no job was too big or too small. If I had an idea that I thought might be viewed as controversial, I was careful to keep it to myself. My main focus was on fitting in and being liked. I thought this was the best way for me to get ahead." **Ilene—a Pleaser**

In this particular situation, it seems as though Ilene's personality type matches the needs of the organization. If a Pleaser is employed by a company that values her unquestioning adherence to the company line, she will go far, moving through the ranks to upper management. She is seen as a model employee. But despite all outward appearances, there is a hidden cost. That cost is usually the professional growth and development of the person involved. The patriarchal type of corporate culture and the nonindividuated behavior it favors can have a negative impact on one's sense of self-worth and esteem.

Sarah, a thirty-one-year-old woman who currently works as a marketing assistant for a large retail chain, is another variation on the Pleaser role. Sarah's parents died in an accident when she was very young, and her aunt and uncle raised her. Despite their reassurance and love, Sarah grew up feeling insecure and afraid that if she did something wrong, she would be abandoned. In order to fit in and be loved, Sarah was very helpful and cooperative. She did whatever was asked of her and constantly sought ways of pleasing the members of her new family. This type of behavior has continued into her work life; however, her desire to please often exceeds her ability to follow through on the task.

Sarah has been an employee of her present company for about a year. Prior to this job, she worked in the marketing department of a clothing manufacturer. Her work history has been marked by short-term employment with various companies. Sarah is a friendly and outgoing young woman who promptly immerses herself in her job and the company in which she works. She is chameleon-like in the way she quickly embraces the ideas, philosophy, and working style of her colleagues and superiors. Her Pleaser style is exemplified by her willingness to take on whatever is assigned to her, regardless of her understanding of the task or the time she has available to adequately complete the job. This behavior is motivated by her need to gain the acceptance and approval of her coworkers and superiors. Receiving the positive regard of her colleagues enables her to feel good about herself.

> "I find that I am always into pleasing others. I say things that people want to hear. I do whatever is asked of me, and at times I even sound as though I like it. I am continually stressed. I tend to get involved in too many things. I must learn to say 'no.' "
>
> **Sarah—a Pleaser**

Sarah's eagerness to be a valuable member of the organization is duly noted and she soon finds herself involved in many projects, having said "yes" whenever she is asked to take on another responsibility. After a short time, her good intentions come face-to-face with the reality that she has taken on more than she can handle. Still eager for the goodwill of her coworkers and superiors, Sarah does not acknowledge that she has taken on too much. Instead she begins a pattern of stalling and avoidance behavior. When asked about the progress of a project, she says it is coming along but she needs a little more time. The truth is, however, that she has not even started on the project. After missing a deadline, she has multiple excuses and primarily blames others for not providing her with the information she needed in a timely fashion. Her work behavior is marked by eagerness to take on responsibility coupled with difficulty in seeing projects through to completion.

After repeatedly missing deadlines and not fulfilling commitments, Sarah is seen as undependable. Her behavior then has a negative impact upon her relationships with her bosses and coworkers. She creates problems and alienates people in the office. Her direct supervisors become angry and frustrated with her. Coworkers are upset that they were first made to look bad by her eagerness to volunteer for everything and then have to clean up the problems she creates because of her lack of dependability. Sarah soon loses the trust and high regard she so desperately seeks in order to feel good about herself. Her work relationships become strained, and in time, she leaves the company.

Ilene and Sarah present interesting perspectives of the Pleaser role. While they both engage in behaviors associated with the role, they achieve varying results. This is due in large part to their differing abilities to follow through on responsibilities and finish their tasks.

Ilene has found a good fit for her style of functioning. Her dedication, compliance, and industriousness serve her well. The secret to Ilene's success is not in just taking on additional responsibility but, more important, in following through on whatever she begins. Her goal was to become a valued member of her company. Through hard work and elevating everyone else's needs above her own, she earns the reputation of a loyal company person and is appropriately rewarded. Through her success at work, Ilene feels valued and worthy, feelings she is unable to generate on her own without external validation. In addition, Ilene's behavior enables her to have positive relationships with all her coworkers, thus facilitating a sense of connection in the workplace.

Sarah, on the other hand, struggles with many issues. She desperately wants to be liked and accepted, and to that end, she immerses herself in the culture and social structure of the workplace. She eagerly takes on more responsibility with little or no thought about how she will accomplish all she has agreed to do. Her need to feel valued by her colleagues dominates her thinking, and Sarah continues to overextend herself. Her inability to follow through on her commitments results in strained relationships and a lack of external validation from coworkers and superiors.

Ilene and Sarah are both motivated to be Pleasers because of their insecurities. They require external validation to compensate for what they are unable to provide for themselves. Both of these women have many strengths; however, due to their earlier experiences, neither has developed a clear picture of her identity as a capable adult person. Both women, like most Pleasers, have spent most of their lives focused on others, which left them little time or energy to become aware of, or give voice to, their own thoughts and needs.

The Relationship Between Self-Concept and Behavior

In the cases of both Ilene and Sarah, their ideas about themselves have a significant impact upon their behaviors. Both women have not developed a clear picture of who they are as individuals and consequently believe that their only value is to be found in the eyes of others. In order to change their behaviors, they first have to identify the thoughts that maintain the Pleaser role.

If you identify with the Pleaser role in any way, the following Work Role Exercise may help increase your own awareness. Its purpose is threefold: (1) to identify the thoughts that maintain your role; (2) to change your thinking, which will then change your behavior; and (3) to create a plan for changing your behavior.

Pleaser Work Role Exercise

1. **What thoughts do you have about yourself that maintain the role of the Pleaser?**

    _____

    _____

2. **What evidence supports these thoughts?**

    _____

    _____

3. **What evidence disputes these thoughts?**

    _____

    _____

4. **What alternative behavior(s) would you like to exhibit?**

    _____

    _____

5. **What steps must you take in the short term (3–6 months) to progress toward this new behavior?**

Step 1 _____

Step 2 _____

Step 3 _____

6. **What steps must you take in the long term (1–3 years) to progress toward this new behavior?**

Step 1 _____

Step 2 _____

Step 3 _____

7. **What thoughts may interfere with your taking these steps?**

_____

_____

8. **What would you tell a friend who shared these concerns with you? Write down this alternative perspective and use it to motivate yourself to start changing your behavior.**

_____

_____

• • •

Conclusion

Two major traps for Pleasers are the possibilities that other people may take advantage of them and that they may accept more responsibilities than they can fulfill. A Pleaser commonly finds herself in situations in which her desire to please is exploited. It can be painful for the Pleaser to realize that she has been used, rather than accepted and valued as part of a team. She may then feel even more devalued and insecure, which may lead to depression. Pleasers who agree to everything and accomplish little create strained working relationships that are exactly the opposite of the acceptance and validation they seek. Both of these traps undermine the professional development of the Pleaser. In this chapter, our goals were to make you aware of the characteristic behaviors of the Pleaser and to help you formulate a plan for change. If you want to change your behavior, you must first become aware of it. For most of us, our behavior is so automatic that we are not even aware of what we are doing. You can initiate change by using the exercises in this chapter and by identifying the behaviors you would like to stop, start, and continue.

THE PLEASER: A PLAN OF ACTION

Stop	Subjugating your own needs to the need of others
	Overextending yourself to gain the approval of others
Start	Valuing yourself
	Recognizing your strengths
	Understanding and meeting your own needs
Continue	Being sensitive to the needs of others
	Being a good worker, diligent, and cooperative
	Developing healthy, positive relationships with coworkers

The Pleaser's primary strengths include selflessness and consideration for the needs of others. Although attending to the needs of others is certainly a trait to be admired, it is the degree to which the Pleaser focuses on pleasing others that is problematic. Continually subordinating your own needs to the needs of others so that they will like, accept, and value you inhibits your own growth. Balancing your needs with the needs of others is the key to change. Become aware of the strengths and characteristics you possess in order to attain a clearer sense of who you are, develop a more positive self-image, and create a winning role.

"My role as a child was to take care of my mother, brother, and sister. Taking care of people and solving problems is what I do best."

5   ROLE OF THE CAREGIVER

These are the words Rachel used to describe her role as a child in her family and as an adult. For Rachel and others who occupy the Caregiver role, the goal is to take care of everyone around them and create a sense of closeness with the people in their lives. This role typically results when a child assumes adult responsibilities within the family, and it is often reinforced by the praise the child receives for her adultlike behaviors. Phrases such as "he's the man of the house" or "she takes such good care of her sister and brother—she's like a little mommy" encourage a child to take on more and more responsibility in return for more acknowledgment.

These behaviors become an integral part of the Caregiver's identity and are brought forward into all aspects of her adult life.

Workplace Behaviors

The Caregiver can be characterized as a person who takes on total responsibility for the wants, needs, and problems of others. At work, the Caregiver often becomes the mother hen, laboring diligently to ensure that morale is high, people are heard, and everyone's needs are being met. The Caregiver becomes immersed in her coworkers' problems and strives tirelessly to help solve them. Given the Caregiver's long history of problem solving and taking charge, she can often appear headstrong or stubborn because she believes she knows what is right. When others do not agree with her observations or reject her help, she becomes upset and frustrated. Since helping others has been a way of eliciting praise and positive attention, any rejection of her attempts may feel like a complete rejection of her as a person. She may then react with anger or withdrawal.

There are both positive and negative aspects associated with the role of the Caregiver at work. Positive aspects include her ability to listen and observe; she is very attuned to her environment. As a result of her years of experience, the Caregiver is adept at identifying problems and finding appropriate solutions. Her ability to solve problems in a calm and thorough manner is a valuable resource in a fast-paced work setting. The Caregiver is reliable. This makes her a natural "go to" person, the one others look to for help when they have a question or a problem at work. She is also very generous about sharing with her coworkers whatever she has learned. The Caregiver is proficient at creating a sense of community or family within her work environment.

The negative aspects of the role include her excessive sense of responsibility when dealing with work and interpersonal situations. She tends to accept all of the blame for negative situations and seldom if ever acknowledges that other people might also be responsible. Given this perspective, it is easy to understand why the Caregiver invests so much of herself in solving the problems that arise in the course of her work. Yet the tendency to be overly involved in everything that is happening in the office takes a tremendous toll on her. She is always under stress, and this in turn may produce physical symptoms that undermine her ability to do her best. The Caregiver has never learned to set limits in either her work or her personal life; she has a hard time saying "no" when asked to do something. These factors often lead to burnout.

THE CAREGIVER: CHARACTER SUMMARY

Strengths	Weaknesses
Sensitive to needs of others	Feels overly responsible for problems of others
Good listening skills	Unable to set limits
Aware of environment	Opinionated
Good at collecting and sharing information	Develops physical symptoms as a result of stress and inability to control all situations
Problem solver	Vulnerable to burnout
Cares about others	Needs to be in control
Reliable and dependable	Inflexible

Caregiver Self-Evaluation

Now that you have read over the general characteristics, both positive and negative, of the Caregiver, can you identify with this role?

_____

If so, what behaviors of the Caregiver role do you engage in?

_____

Have the behaviors of the Caregiver role enhanced your success? If so, how?

_____

_____

Have the behaviors of the Caregiver role hindered your success? If so, how?

_____

_____

•   •   •

The Caregiver is extremely sensitive to her environment, especially to the needs of others and the role she plays with regard to those needs. It is helpful to think of the Caregiver's behavior on a continuum representing her sensitivity to the environment. Sensitivity to the environment includes sensitivity to others, such as her boss, coworkers, and staff; sensitivity to company culture; and sensitivity to self. It is important to note that being sensitive to the needs of others is not negative in itself; rather, it is the degree to which the Caregiver engages in those behaviors that determines whether the consequence is negative, and hinders success, or positive, and facilitates success.

If you can identify with the role of the Caregiver, take a moment to rate your sensitivity to others, to company culture, and to self on the following continua. You can then determine for yourself if your sensitivity and behaviors are helpful to your career.

Sensitivity to Environment Exercise

0% = Least sensitivity   100% = Greatest sensitivity

1. People: Sensitivity to Others

0%	10	20	30	40	50	60	70	80	90	100%

2. Culture: Sensitivity to Company Culture

0%	10	20	30	40	50	60	70	80	90	100%

3. Self: Sensitivity to Self

0%	10	20	30	40	50	60	70	80	90	100%

• • •

If an individual shows no sensitivity to the needs of coworkers, she would be at the 0% end of the Sensitivity to Others scale and would probably be experiencing continuous difficulties at work. This type of behavior would almost certainly sabotage her professional success. Likewise, if she disregards the culture of the company and persistently opposes its usual way of doing things, she would be at 0% on the Sensitivity to Company Culture scale and would again be hampering her ability to succeed at work. The Caregiver usually falls somewhere in the 80% to 100% range on the Sensitivity to Others and Sensitivity to Company Culture scales. The 80% to 100% range indicates a disproportionate focus on the needs of others and on company culture; this diminishes the Caregiver's ability to succeed professionally and often leads to burnout.

On the other hand, the Caregiver typically falls in the 0% to 20% range on the Sensitivity to Self scale. We attribute this range to her tendency to be overly responsible as a way of getting positive feedback and maintaining close relationships with her coworkers.

Identifying where your behaviors fall on the above scales will heighten your awareness of how you function within your work environment. You can then decide whether your behaviors are valued by your organization and are putting you on the right track for success or if your company is taking advantage of you and passing you over for promotions. Companies that value aggression and competitiveness often are not impressed with a person who is considerate, a troubleshooter, and willing to quietly assume more and more responsibility in the spirit of helping others. For this reason, the Caregiver probably will not be promoted or viewed as an up-and-comer. Instead, she is used and pigeonholed in the role she currently occupies.

The Caregiver must take the time to identify her needs and how her behaviors fit within the culture of the company. Applying a more balanced perspective to the three elements related to sensitivity to the environment would enable the Caregiver to acknowledge and integrate her needs for growth with the needs of the organization. This balance of people, culture, and self will lead to greater success for all concerned. The goal is to reach 50% to 60% on each of the three scales. This balanced way of functioning is a healthier alternative to the Caregiver's excessive sense of responsibility and will lead to individual professional growth and success.

Two Styles of the Caregiver Role

As with all of these roles, there are different ways of functioning as a Caregiver, which vary according to the personality of the individual. We will now take a more detailed look at how the Caregiver role developed and plays out for two women, Rachel and Sally.

Rachel is a warm and competent thirty-year-old woman who is working as a sales manager for an insurance company. She developed the role of the Caregiver

> "I look upon my coworkers as a family and consequently am very invested in their success and well-being. I have given much thought and attention to what works in this company, and I share this knowledge with my staff. I feel very strongly about the direction and advice I give them with regard to handling situations and problems."

Rachel—a Caregiver

as a child when she took on parenting responsibilities for her brother and sister after her mother became ill following a divorce.

In her professional life, Rachel is the mother figure, taking care of people as she has done throughout her life. She believes she knows what is best in various situations and is quite direct in getting her message across. Despite her maternal solicitude, she can be extremely assertive and does not back down from conflict. Her coworkers have mixed reactions to her; some respect her opinions and value her style, while others believe she is too abrupt and stubborn. The colleagues who respect her seek her out for her problem-solving skills and unique perspective, while others find her blunt, domineering, and sometimes confrontational. Although she may listen to her coworkers, she has already formed her opinion and can be unwavering, even aggressive, in its defense. Rachel assumes the role of the strong leader because she believes she knows what is best. When things do not work out as she expects, she becomes upset and often takes it personally.

The following vignette illustrates a typical work situation for Rachel. While working on a certain project, Rachel's job was to go from group to group to collect information about what each one was doing. She was then supposed to put it into a newsletter to keep the rest of the company informed. When people did not give her the information she needed in a timely fashion, she became very frustrated and took the lack of cooperation personally.

Rachel's style has both helped and hindered her in the workplace. She is sensitive to the needs of the company and her colleagues. She spends a lot of time training new employees and familiarizing them with the culture of the company. Because of her dedication and hard work, she is seen as the troubleshooter and problem solver who can handle anything she is given. However, her inability to set limits and focus on her own career goals has undermined her professional standing in the company and stalled her climb up the corporate ladder. It is important to note that although being available for your coworkers is positive, overdoing it can have negative consequences. Rachel has learned this the hard way. She drives herself so hard that she forgoes sleep in order to squeeze one more task or responsibility into her already full day. This lessens her ability to see a project through to completion without getting sick or becoming completely stressed-out.

Rachel has been working on creating more balance between her sensitivity to others, her company, and herself. She realizes that her extreme focus on the needs of others has left her little time and energy to recognize and attend to her own needs. Rachel has identified her professional goal and developed a plan to attain it. While she continues to be a solicitous and helpful individual, she has learned to set limits on the tasks she accepts so that she can complete projects on time and without compromising her health. She is more astute politically and has identified which attributes are valued by the company and the right people with whom to ally herself. She is working on strengthening her leadership abilities by continuing to use her strong communication skills and balancing her concern for others with concern for herself.

Sally, a forty-five-year-old social worker in a large urban hospital, represents a more aggressive Caregiver. She grew up with an alcoholic mother and an emotionally abusive father. As the oldest daughter, Sally's role was to take care of her siblings and her mother, who was often too drunk to be responsible for herself. Sally learned to survive in this chaotic household by being very aware of the needs of her family members and doing everything within her power to meet them. Her desire to be a social worker was a natural outgrowth of her childhood. Working in a hospital setting, she interacts continually with hospital administrators, physicians, patients, and patients' families in order to meet the needs of the patients.

In addition to the gratification she receives from her nurturing behaviors, the Caregiver role also gives Sally a sense of control over her life. However, when people do not follow her suggestions, this sense of control is threatened, and Sally becomes angry, even verbally abusive at times. She responds by becoming even more forceful in her approach, which has led to strained relationships with many of her colleagues. So although Sally is an intelligent and resourceful woman, many of her colleagues choose to work around her rather than become entangled in her belligerent style and angry outbursts. Sally believes she is

> "I have been taking care of others since I was very young, and I believe I am good at what I do. I put a lot of energy into finding the right solutions for patients and their families, and I often have to be very strong in order to get all those concerned to support the best solution to the situation."
>
> **Sally—a Caregiver**

putting all her energy into helping people to help themselves, but in fact, her behavior is a way of getting the acknowledgment she needs in order to feel good about herself.

When her help is rejected, she often feels as though she herself is being rejected, and this makes her angry and frustrated. Over time, Sally has internalized much of her feelings and has developed chronic gastrointestinal problems.

Sally and Rachel present interesting aspects of the Caregiver role. While both focus on being available to help other people, Sally's underlying anger seems to dominate her response when her assistance is not accepted. This anger then results in resentment and strained working relationships that are detrimental to Sally's professional aspirations. Rachel, although domineering at times, does not have the same emotional difficulties as Sally, and when things do not go as planned, she redoubles her efforts to help others in any way she can. As we have stated previously, Rachel's intense focus on being available to others at the expense of her own well-being frequently results in burnout and difficulty in finishing her own projects on time. On the other hand, Rachel can always be counted on to get things done, but the frantic pace and tension that result from bringing projects in right under the wire has blocked her advancement at work. So although each woman differs in the way she carries out her Caregiver role, the result is the same with regard to professional success.

Both Rachel and Sally were brought up with the belief that they must always be there for others, and they have brought this requirement into all aspects of their lives. Unfortunately, this idea is also tied up with other self-concepts that have led to problems for both women. In Rachel's case, her self-image revolves around giving to others with no concern for herself. She believes that if she wants to be a mature, responsible individual she must take on the problems of her coworkers and those she cares about. Saying "no," setting limits on what she is reasonably able to do, and considering her own needs are contrary to her idea of what a responsible person should do. Sally's sense of responsibility to others is tied to her chaotic childhood experiences. She feels that if people reject her help, they are rejecting her and devaluing her as an individual. This devaluation and rejection then trigger Sally's anger. Caregiver behaviors can be positive, but as we can see in the brief descriptions of Rachel's and Sally's work experiences, it can be detrimental to professional success.

The Relationship Between Self-Concept and Behavior

For both Rachel and Sally, their past ideas about themselves and their responsibilities produced a significant impact on their behaviors. Before they can create a more integrated and balanced approach in their work, they have to become aware of the thoughts that maintain their current ways of functioning.

The following Work Role Exercise is one method of increasing awareness of your thoughts. The purpose of this exercise is threefold: (1) to identify the thoughts that maintain your role; (2) to change your thinking, which will then change your behavior; and (3) to create a plan for changing your behavior.

Caregiver Work Role Exercise

1. **What thoughts do you have about yourself that maintain the role of the Caregiver?**

   _____

   _____

2. **What evidence supports these thoughts?**

   _____

   _____

3. **What evidence disputes these thoughts?**

   _____

   _____

4. **What alternative behavior(s) would you like to exhibit?**

   _____

   _____

5. **What steps must you take in the short term (3–6 months) to progress toward this new behavior?**

Step 1 _____

Step 2 _____

Step 3 _____

6. **What steps must you take in the long term (1–3 years) to progress toward this new behavior?**

    Step 1 _____

    Step 2 _____

    Step 3 _____

7. **What thoughts may interfere with your taking these steps?**

    _____

    _____

8. **What would you tell a friend who shared these concerns with you? Write down this alternative perspective and use it to motivate yourself to start changing your behavior.**

    _____

    _____

• • •

Conclusion

One major trap for the Caregiver is that in concentrating on the needs of others, she leaves her own needs unmet and her dreams unrealized. Her lack of focus on her own career development hinders her progress and can lead to frustration and sometimes hopelessness. This frustration may be played out as friction between the Caregiver and her boss or between the Caregiver and her coworkers. It is also important for the Caregiver to remember that in order to create good working relationships with her coworkers, their contacts should be characterized by cooperation and respect, not the dictatorial phrases she was forced to use as a child when adult responsibilities were thrust upon her.

The role of the Caregiver contains many strengths and positive behaviors. While it is certainly admirable to be unfailingly available for others, trouble arises when the needs of the Caregiver are out of balance with the needs of others. It is not the behavior itself that is negative; rather, it is the degree to which the Caregiver engages in that behavior that causes problems. Changing our behavior requires that we first become aware of it. For most of us, our behavior is so automatic that we are not even aware of what we are doing. You can implement change by using the exercises in this chapter and by identifying the behaviors you would like to stop, start, and continue.

THE CAREGIVER: A PLAN OF ACTION

Stop	Overextending yourself
	Being overly responsible for others
	Trying to control everything
	Getting angry when others do not follow your directions
Start	Balancing your own needs with the needs of others
	Focusing on your own career
	Communicating with others in a respectful, adult manner
Continue	Being concerned for others
	Being a problem solver
	Being dependable

To succeed professionally, the Caregiver must create a more balanced perspective by recognizing her own needs, identifying the behaviors that are valued by the company, and integrating her needs with the needs of others and the company culture. Through this process, the Caregiver will be able to use the strengths she possesses to redirect her focus, enhance her career, and develop a winning role.

"As a child, I was always being criticized and compared to my brother. I was never good enough. No one ever listened to me. No one listens to me even now. I'm not worth listening to. I'm worthless."

6   ROLE OF THE SURVIVOR

These are the words Kate used to describe how she felt as a child and how she still feels as an adult. For Kate and others who have taken on the role of the Survivor, the goal is to adapt to the situations in which they find themselves. A Survivor who works to recognize her strengths and discard the negative ideas she has about herself will enhance her chances for success in the workplace.

The Survivor is characterized by her belief that she has little or no control over the events in her life and that the best she can do is try to get by without failing completely. This belief has a detrimental effect on the Survivor's views of herself and the world. Even though she has many strengths, which she has already demonstrated, she discounts them. She chooses to see only her shortcomings.

Workplace Behaviors

Because of her negative attitude, the Survivor often relinquishes any control she might otherwise have over her environment. Despite the pain and unhappiness she may be feeling inside, the Survivor presents herself as a kind and friendly person around the office. She works hard and hopes that her efforts will please her superiors, but she is always on the lookout for criticism. The Survivor often gravitates to jobs with critical and demanding employers, where she repeats her earlier difficult relationships. These experiences prove to the Survivor that she is not good enough, not worthy, and has no choice but simply to adapt.

There are both positive and negative aspects associated with the role of the Survivor at work. Positive aspects include her ability to adapt to situations and environments of all kinds. She is able to pull herself together and function well in demanding positions regardless of her emotional state. Her work is important to her and she always tries to do the best job she possibly can in order to prove to herself and to others that she is good enough. She is dependable and responsible and repeatedly demonstrates these qualities in all aspects of her life. The Survivor is a strong woman, and it is this strength that enables her to persevere in spite of her difficulties.

Negative aspects of the role include her tendency to acquiesce to the needs and dictates of others, thereby disregarding her own rights and needs. The Survivor often feels helpless when faced with difficult situations. This is due in large part to her negative belief that she is incapable of changing her life, which results in resignation, the surrender of any control she may possess, and self-pity. She concentrates on how to cope with and survive existing situations and has little if any energy left over to grow as an individual. The Survivor tends to personalize the comments and behaviors of others and interprets most of them in a negative fashion. She lives her life reactively, waiting for things to happen to her instead of making things happen. This behavior demonstrates her feelings of powerlessness. When working with others, she is submissive and vulnerable. She rarely questions their dictates and puts much energy into meeting their requests in an effort to avoid conflict and criticism.

THE SURVIVOR: CHARACTER SUMMARY

Strengths	Weaknesses
Strong	Vulnerable
Able to persevere	Personalizes
Copes with all types of situations	Reactive
Compassionate	Surrenders control of her life
Team player	Fears the unknown
Agreeable	Negative beliefs about herself
Responsible	Fears failure

Survivor Self-Evaluation

Now that you have read over the general characteristics, both positive and negative, of the Survivor, can you identify with this role?

If so, what behaviors of the Survivor role do you engage in?

Have the behaviors of the Survivor role enhanced your success? If so, how?

Have the behaviors of the Survivor role hindered your success? If so, how?

• • •

The Survivor is extremely sensitive to her environment. She concentrates continually on doing more than what is expected of her because meeting the needs of others makes her feel worthy. It is helpful to think of the Survivor's behavior on a scale. Sensitivity to the environment includes sensitivity to others, such as boss, coworkers, and staff; sensitivity to company culture; and sensitivity to self. The Survivor's sensitivity to her environment is a positive characteristic of the role. Problems arise when she concentrates exclusively on others and disregards herself. It is this skewed perspective that presents a problem. The following scales are designed to help you understand that it is not necessarily the behavior that is good or bad; rather, it is the degree to which one engages in the behavior that determines whether the consequence is negative, and hinders success, or positive, and facilitates success.

If you can identify with the role of the Survivor, then take a moment to rate your sensitivity to others, to company culture, and to self on the following scales. You can then determine for yourself how helpful your sensitivity and behaviors are to your career.

Sensitivity to Environment Exercise

0% = Least sensitivity   100% = Greatest sensitivity

1. People: Sensitivity to Others

0%	10	20	30	40	50	60	70	80	90	100%

2. Culture: Sensitivity to Company Culture

0%	10	20	30	40	50	60	70	80	90	100%

3. Self: Sensitivity to Self

0%	10	20	30	40	50	60	70	80	90	100%

• • •

If an individual shows no sensitivity to the needs of coworkers, she would be at the 0% end of the Sensitivity to Others scale and would be experiencing continual difficulties at work. This type of behavior would almost certainly sabotage her professional success. Likewise, if she disregards the culture of the company and persistently works in opposition to its usual procedures, she would be at 0% on the Sensitivity to Company Culture scale and would again be sabotaging her ability to succeed at work. The Survivor usually falls somewhere in the 80% to 100% range on the Sensitivity to Others scale. The 80% to 100% range indicates a disproportionate focus on the needs of others, which may undermine her ability to grow and develop her own position within the company. Given her insecurities and need to feel worthy, her sensitivity to her coworkers is somewhat greater than her sensitivity to the company culture. She tends to personalize and focus on the behaviors of people because they are more discernible than the ambiguous corporate culture. As a result, her range of 60% to 80% on the Sensitivity to Company Culture scale is somewhat lower than her range on the Sensitivity to Others scale.

On the other hand, the Survivor typically falls in the 0% to 20% range on the Sensitivity to Self scale, due to her tendency to be overly concerned with meeting everyone else's needs as a means of compensating for her own insecurities. While the need to balance each of the three elements is great, the Survivor's first priority should be herself. She must identify what her needs are and express them. She must give herself permission to articulate her ideas and stand up for herself.

A more balanced focus on the three elements related to sensitivity to the environment would allow the Survivor to acknowledge and integrate her own needs for growth with the needs of the organization. This balance of people, culture, and self will result in great success for all concerned. The goal is to strive for 50% to 60% on each of the three scales. This will lead to a more balanced way of functioning and is a healthier alternative to the Survivor's tendency to devalue herself in the workplace. This more balanced sensitivity will increase her potential for professional success.

Two Styles of the Survivor Role

There are Survivors in every workplace. These are the people who show up every day, try their best, but often feel that they can never get ahead. Perhaps you can identify with some of the characteristics of the Survivor, or you may work with someone who fits the role. We will now take a look at how this role plays out in the work lives of two women, Kate and Peg.

Kate is a twenty-eight-year-old administrative assistant in a large information technology company. She grew up in a middle-class family in a small town with her mother, father, and older brother. As a child, she had a great deal of difficulty in school and thought of herself as stupid. Her teachers and parents believed she was just lazy and continuously criticized her and punished her for not doing well in school. Much later, it was determined that Kate's problems were caused by a learning disability, which was then treated. But after years of living with her undiagnosed learning problem and incessant comparisons to her academically successful brother, Kate believed she was inadequate and had become very withdrawn. She felt powerless and concentrated on just getting through each day. Kate continues to feel this way in her personal life as well as at work.

Today Kate finds herself in a difficult work environment, in a male-dominated field under the supervision of a demanding, aggressive boss. She manages to survive by relinquishing all of her rights and doing whatever she is asked to do as quickly and as well as possible in order to avoid verbal abuse from her boss. She is submissive and accepts whatever work or blame is thrown at her; she is too fearful to stand up for herself and feels overwhelmed by a sense of powerlessness.

The following vignette illustrates the powerlessness Kate feels at work. Last week, when her boss was critical of work she had completed, she became upset but chose not to respond in any way. Kate is very intimidated by those in upper management. She is always afraid that they will ultimately find something wrong with her work and fire her. As a result, she hesitates to speak up, believing that her best course of action is to do as she is told and stay with the program.

> "Although working here is very unpleasant and difficult, I'm afraid to leave because I may not find another job that pays as well. I'm also not good at certain things, and another employer might get even more frustrated with me than my present boss. It looks like I'm stuck here, so I might as well just hold my breath and get through each day."
>
> **Kate—a Survivor**

Kate retreats when confronted with behaviors that she interprets as overwhelming and impossible to handle. She focuses on not making waves, not making any demands, because she feels unworthy; she believes she has no right to express her views or expect her needs to be met.

Kate's pessimism and fear of the unknown keep her stuck in a position where she is constantly criticized and demeaned, not unlike the way she was treated as a child. Her hesitancy to speak up and her submissive attitude send a message to others, giving them permission to be disrespectful and sometimes verbally abusive. The demanding, nonsupportive culture of the company activates Kate's negative image of herself. This weakens her ability to cope with the requirements of her job, which intensifies her sense of inadequacy. In an effort to conceal her emotions, Kate presents herself as easygoing, solicitous, and agreeable to anyone who asks anything of her, yet she often feels isolated and alone.

Kate is highly sensitive to criticism and tends to personalize the statements and behaviors of others. She interprets many of the comments of her coworkers and boss in a negative way. These misunderstandings

"I start each day resigned to dealing with whatever comes my way and reassuring myself that I can handle things. I nevertheless feel somewhat anxious that my luck will run out at any time. I feel as though I am wearing a mask, smiling on the outside, yet scared and alone on the inside." **Kate—a Survivor**

often lead to troubled work relationships despite her best efforts to appear agreeable and cooperative. Kate is a strong young woman who manages to persevere; however, the cost of her self-doubt and feelings of inadequacy is high. She puts more energy into hiding what she believes are her shortcomings than into developing and growing professionally. Because of this imbalance, Kate has frequently been passed over for promotions.

Peg is a thirty-five-year-old paralegal at a midsize law firm. She is the divorced mother of two children. Peg's parents were divorced when she was ten years old, and her mother raised her and her older sister. Peg's mother was an angry, domineering woman; she was frustrated about the way her life had turned out and took it out on her children. She punished them for the smallest infraction and continually criticized their behavior. Peg and her sister grew up trying to figure out their mother's moods and how to avoid being hollered at and punished. They walked on eggshells in an effort to get

"I used to think of things I could do that would make Mom like me. I was sure if I were just better at helping around the house, or better at school, Mom would be nicer to me. I remember studying hard to do well in school, but no matter what grades I brought home, Mom would always find something to criticize. I was sure Mom didn't like me because I was a disappointment to her." **Peg—a Survivor**

some positive attention. As a child, Peg did not realize that her mother's treatment of her was not based on how good or bad she was, and she began to believe there was something wrong with her.

Because of these constant negative interactions with her mother, Peg began to believe she was inadequate and worthless. She never realized that her mother's behavior rose out of her own inability to deal with the anger and frustration she felt after her divorce many years before. Peg was convinced that there was something unworthy about her and kept trying to make up for what she perceived as her deficiencies.

To escape from her mother's house, Peg married young and had two children. After a short period of time, Peg's husband picked up where her mother had left off. He berated her incessantly for the way she took care of the house and was rearing the children. Again, Peg was convinced that she just wasn't good enough, so she tried harder. She chose not to see her husband's shortcomings and instead accepted all the responsibility for whatever was going wrong in their marriage. Her husband began drinking heavily, and the verbal abuse turned into physical abuse. Still, Peg remained in the marriage because she wanted to keep the family together. As the abuse worsened and became a threat to her children, Peg realized that she had no alternative but to leave, and the marriage ended in divorce. Peg went back to work full-time to support herself and her children.

Peg's boss is a very serious man who has a reputation for being difficult. Peg works hard, doing whatever is asked of her cheerfully and efficiently. She wants to prove that she is a good paralegal and that people can depend on her. Despite Peg's best efforts, her boss continually criticizes and demeans her. True to her style, Peg takes on all of the responsibility for her boss's negative behavior. Each time her boss criticizes her, Peg takes a deep breath and waits for him to stop ranting and raving. She then goes off to try to do a better job. She believes that her coworkers consider her inadequate, and because of this, she interprets anything they say as unfavorable. Her tendency to personalize all comments in a negative manner has led Peg to withdraw more and more from her coworkers, leaving her isolated in the midst of a busy office.

The Relationship Between Self-Concept and Behavior

Both Kate and Peg have been victimized by circumstances and see themselves as powerless victims, so they allow others to control their lives and will submit to any kind of treatment. Both women believe they must tolerate the existing circumstances because there is nothing they can do and nowhere for them to go. What they do not realize is that their negative beliefs about themselves, not their lack of ability, have trapped them in unhappy situations. Kate and Peg possess strength and courage, struggling day after day in an uphill battle against their own self-doubt. They are capable, hardworking, intelligent, and compassionate women who bring sensitivity and determination to their work. These women describe themselves as victims; the reality is that they are survivors. They have survived emotional, verbal, and physical abuse, and they have created lives for themselves regardless of the circumstances.

Both women grew up with frequent criticisms of their behavior. For varying reasons, they were belittled by their parents and became the family scapegoats. This pattern continued into their adult lives. They gravitated toward employers who criticized and demeaned them. In so doing, they duplicated both their relationships with their parents and their reactions as children, feeling powerless and withdrawing. They did this, not purposely, but because it was familiar for them on some level. These two women developed negative beliefs about themselves and their ability to stand up for themselves and take control of their lives. The troubled professional and personal relationships in which they participate are a known commodity: they are used to this type of verbal and emotional abuse and know how to react to it.

Kate's and Peg's childhood experiences led to the formation of their negative beliefs about themselves, which in turn affected the quality of their lives. Believing they are inadequate and worthless has led them into unhappy personal and work relationships. In reality, both of these women are strong and intelligent, capable of doing whatever they choose. They have the power to take control of their lives and change their behavior.

If you can identify with the role of the Survivor, the following Work Role Exercise may help you become more aware of your thoughts. The purpose of this exercise is threefold: (1) to identify the thoughts that maintain the role; (2) to change your thinking, which will then change your behavior; and (3) to create a plan for changing your behavior.

Survivor Work Role Exercise

1. **What thoughts do you have about yourself that maintain the role of the Survivor?**

   _____

   _____

2. **What evidence supports these thoughts?**

   _____

   _____

3. **What evidence disputes these thoughts?**

_____

_____

4. **What alternative behavior(s) would you like to exhibit?**

_____

_____

5. **What steps must you take in the short term (3–6 months) to progress toward this new behavior?**

   Step 1 _____

   Step 2 _____

   Step 3 _____

6. **What steps must you take in the long term (1–3 years) to progress toward this new behavior?**

   Step 1 _____

   Step 2 _____

   Step 3 _____

7. **What thoughts may interfere with your taking these steps?**

_____

_____

8. **What would you tell a friend who shared these concerns with you? Write down this alternative perspective and use it to motivate yourself to start changing your behavior.**

_____

_____

• • •

Conclusion

One major trap for the Survivor is the possibility that she will not change, that she will remain unaware of the qualities and strengths she possesses. Another trap is that the Survivor will direct all her energy into serving other people and will never work as diligently to achieve her own growth. The Survivor will benefit from identifying her strengths and believing in herself. Change can be implemented by using the exercises in this chapter and by identifying the behaviors you would like to stop, start, and continue.

THE SURVIVOR: A PLAN OF ACTION

Stop
- Resigning yourself to circumstances
- Feeling hopeless
- Relinquishing control of your life
- Being reactive in most situations
- Personalizing the actions and comments of others
- Allowing others to take advantage of you

Start
- Being more proactive
- Taking more control of your life
- Finding your voice
- Recognizing your strengths
- Identifying your needs
- Developing goals for yourself and a plan to accomplish these goals
- Setting limits in your relationships

Continue
- Being strong
- Persevering by finding ways of coping regardless of the situation
- Caring about others

The Survivor is frequently quick to complain and blame others for her plight. What she does not realize is that she sabotages herself with her behaviors. It is our hope that by using the various exercises in this chapter, the Survivor can gain a greater awareness of herself and begin to see the repetitive patterns in her life. She can then work on changing her perspective, which will in turn lead to a change in behavior. Although life appears bleak to the Survivor, she does possess strengths. Before she can take control of her life and begin to feel more content, she must recognize these strengths and integrate them into her daily life in order to create a winning role.

"I was a very independent and successful child. I always tried to find ways to work around problems and come out okay. When I was nine years old, I sold apples off the tree in my backyard and made it into a little business. I have been creating businesses ever since then."

7 ROLE OF THE ENTREPRENEUR

These are the words Jean used to describe the entrepreneurial attitude she displayed as a child, which she has brought forward in her adult life. For Jean and others who occupy the role of the Entrepreneur, the goal is to achieve and be successful by identifying a need and satisfying it creatively.

The Entrepreneur is characterized by her focus on developing new ideas and finding ways of bringing those ideas to fruition. She does not allow herself to be sidetracked or discouraged by people who disagree with her or try to block her path. Her creativity is enhanced by her enthusiasm for whatever project she has undertaken and her willingness to take risks.

Workplace Behaviors

An Entrepreneur typically is an individual who will create and operate her own company. Whether this business is a start-up that operates out of the home or a larger company that has grown over time, the Entrepreneur always concentrates on developing new ideas, products, and workplace procedures. Creativity and innovation are some of the primary strengths of the Entrepreneur.

Sometimes, the Entrepreneur can be found working as an employee at an already established company. In such a situation, the Entrepreneur may be confronted with a variety of working conditions that will have a significant impact on her success or failure with that employer. Some large companies accept the Entrepreneur's internally driven style more readily than others. They understand that she brings in business and creates strong relationships with colleagues as well as with current and prospective clients. Companies that value the Entrepreneur provide an environment characterized by freedom and support, where she will be unhampered by bureaucratic constraints and hierarchical directives. There are no formal job descriptions or fixed working schedules; instead, the Entrepreneur is allowed to function in the way that suits her best, as long as she does her job, develops new business, and creates innovative programs. Companies that are less supportive of the Entrepreneur's working style attempt to fit her into their established structure and procedures. When the Entrepreneur is forced to function in a defined job, she often feels frustrated and stifled by the limits that are imposed on her. This leads to a difficult working situation that may result in her seeking employment elsewhere.

There are both positive and negative aspects associated with the role of the Entrepreneur at work. Positive aspects include creativity, enthusiasm, and self-confidence. The Entrepreneur is a self-reliant idea person. Whether she is working for herself or for another company, she is able to identify a need that has gone unfilled, then works to develop a way to meet that need. She draws upon her strengths to implement her business ideas. The Entrepreneur is also a hard-working, innovative risk taker. She enjoys being challenged and creating something out of nothing. She is particularly skilled at building relationships both inside and outside of the company. She likes working alone or with others who share the same perspective. To the Entrepreneur, nothing is impossible, and the possibilities are endless. She believes this so strongly that she may be involved in multiple projects, ventures, and businesses simultaneously. Others may see her as a role model of sorts, someone to be studied and emulated.

THE ENTREPRENEUR: CHARACTER SUMMARY

Strengths	Weaknesses
Creative	Impatient
Enthusiastic	Intolerant of the weaknesses of others
Willing to take risks	Has difficulty taking directions from others
Hardworking	Needs to be in control
Self-reliant	Has difficulty working in structured environments
Innovative	Has difficulty working with others
Confident	

Entrepreneur Self-Evaluation

Now that you have read over the general characteristics, both positive and negative, of the Entrepreneur, can you identify with this role?

_____

If so, what behaviors of the Entrepreneur role do you engage in?

_____

Have the behaviors of the Entrepreneur role enhanced your success? If so, how?

_____

_____

Have the behaviors of the Entrepreneur role hindered your success? If so, how?

_____

_____

• • •

Negative aspects of the role include the need to be in control and difficulty with taking directions from and working with others. The Entrepreneur feels stifled in a structured environment that she did not create. It's hard for her to be a team player unless she is also leading the team. The Entrepreneur won't tolerate excuses from people who are unable to do their jobs. At times, her commitment to her work and her single-minded focus on reaching her goal make her insensitive to her coworkers. The Entrepreneur's mind is constantly on the project at hand, and she is usually at least three steps ahead of anyone else who may be trying to work with her. She is so caught up in her own thoughts that she has a hard time slowing down to share them with others. As she tries to communicate her vision and goals, she often comes across as impatient.

It can be lonely being the Entrepreneur. She may harbor an intensity toward her job that is not felt by others, and she has a hard time working with people who do not share her drive. At times, she may feel that no one truly understands her vision and goals, and this leaves her feeling isolated and scared. Given their optimistic bent, many Entrepreneurs regard this as "walking to the beat of their own drum," but other Entrepreneurs take a different view. They may feel frustrated and overwhelmed at being out of step with their colleagues, and such emotions may lead to uncertainty about the work itself. During such times, the Entrepreneur should make an effort to connect with others who share her vision and goals.

In terms of her sensitivity to the work environment, the Entrepreneur presents an interesting picture. The Entrepreneur's main goal is to accomplish the project or task she has laid out for herself. She may work alone or with others. She may be working in concert with the company culture or in conflict with it. Her coworkers and the company culture are not her prime concerns. Therefore, her sensitivity to those facets of her environment vary, depending on how they affect the success of her project. It may be helpful to think about the Entrepreneur's behavior on a scale that illustrates her degree of sensitivity to the needs of others, to the company culture, and to her own needs.

The following scales are designed to increase your awareness of the sensitivity you display in the different areas of your workplace. This may help you determine whether the consequences of your behavior are negative, and hinder your success, or positive, and facilitate your success. If you can identify with the role of the Entrepreneur, take a moment to rate your sensitivity to others, company culture, and self on the following scales. You should then be able to determine for yourself how helpful your sensitivity and behaviors are to your career.

Sensitivity to Environment Exercise

0% = Least sensitivity   100% = Greatest sensitivity

1. People: Sensitivity to Others

0%	10	20	30	40	50	60	70	80	90	100%

2. Culture: Sensitivity to Company Culture

0%	10	20	30	40	50	60	70	80	90	100%

3. Self: Sensitivity to Self

0%	10	20	30	40	50	60	70	80	90	100%

● ● ●

If an individual shows no sensitivity to the needs of coworkers, she would be at the 0% end of the Sensitivity to Others scale and would be experiencing continual difficulties at work. This type of behavior would almost certainly sabotage her ability to achieve professional success. Likewise, if she disregards the culture of the company and persistently opposes its standard procedures, she would be at the 0% end of the Sensitivity to Company Culture scale and would again be decreasing her chances to be successful at work. The Entrepreneur usually falls somewhere in the 50% to 60% range on the Sensitivity to Others and Sensitivity to Company Culture scales. This is due to her focus. She is aware of the company culture and the needs of others but does not feel constrained by them. Her goal takes precedence. This behavior is different from the Maverick's because it is not an act of rebellion nor is it specifically aimed at disregarding the culture or the needs of others. Instead, the Entrepreneur is driven only by her desire to succeed and accomplish her goal, and all other issues take a backseat. The Maverick is dedicated to getting her own way, and she will sometimes sacrifice success in order to get it. The Entrepreneur, on the other hand, is interested in success, and the drive to achieve her goal dictates her behavior. Given this perspective, the Entrepreneur works with the culture and is sensitive to the needs of others when these factors are not in conflict with the completion of her project. When conflict does arise, she will listen to the viewpoints of others and present her position in an attempt to find some middle ground where they can all work together. However, if she is unable to gain the support of her coworkers, she will not compromise her beliefs and her position when it comes to achieving her goal.

Due to her inner strength, the belief she has in herself and in her ideas, the Entrepreneur falls within the 80% to 100% range on the Sensitivity to Self scale. The Entrepreneur is particularly sensitive to self because so much of her identity is tied up in her work. She and her work are one and the same. If she is successful, that means her business succeeds, and if her business is successful, she succeeds personally. The fulfillment of her own ideas, vision, and goals are the primary indicators of her professional satisfaction and success.

Two Styles of the Entrepreneur Role

The role of the Entrepreneur varies to some degree depending upon the specific work setting. The Entrepreneur who is running her own business has more freedom to do as she pleases. However, the Entrepreneur who is employed by a company must find a way to maintain her creativity and spirit while functioning in a place where she does not have the last word. We will now take a more detailed look at how the Entrepreneur role develops and is played out with two women, Jean and Nancy.

"I found an excellent job. I had given them my best friend as a reference, and she told them she believed I would do a wonderful job even though I had multiple sclerosis. That was the kiss of death. At that point, I decided that if I couldn't get a job, I would start my own company, and that is what I did."

Jean—an Entrepreneur

Jean is the fifty-eight-year-old founder and chief executive officer of a home health-care agency. She grew up in a poor family with her mother, father, and younger sister. She says her father was her role model and her greatest supporter. He was an engineer and an inventor, and Jean has inherited his daring and courageous spirit. He encouraged her to challenge herself and find ways to accomplish her goals. This independent and creative spirit has marked Jean's life.

As a young woman, she studied business and planned to pursue a career in the business world. However, she had to alter her plans when she married a young minister. Even though her life changed and she assumed the role of a minister's wife, Jean still found ways of being an entrepreneur. First, she developed a reading clinic for children. Then she started a few small businesses to make a little extra money for her family while at the same time satisfying her need to be an entrepreneur.

When her husband was assigned to a large church in a new community, the idea for her current business was born. She knew church members who were ill and needed someone with them in their homes, especially in the evenings, to help them with their basic needs. She began an overnight sitting service and enlisted seminary students as sitters. That was the start of her current company, which has grown to forty-seven offices.

Jean has developed a large and flourishing company because she was able to identify a need that had to be filled. She is a successful but demanding manager.

The following vignette illustrates Jean's entrepreneurial spirit. Jean has an open-door management style that encourages continual interaction between herself and the rest of her staff. As her disease progressed, Jean was faced with the challenge of maintaining her management style. She did this in a way that exemplifies her entrepreneurial creativity. When she started her company, she was able to get out and visit staff members at the different offices. But as the disease progressed, she was unable to get around as she had before. Because she wants to maintain her hands-on open-door policy, she now invites staff members to visit her in the home office on a regular basis. These meetings keep her informed about the weekly operations of several of her branches. She maintains relationships with all forty-seven offices by bringing staff members in for training on a regular basis. She also continues to be directly involved with the company by requiring all new employees to spend one week training with her in her home office. Faced with the same circumstances, another woman might have given up. Jean's entrepreneurial spirit did not allow her to give up.

> "I was looking for a niche that no one else had found, not a medical service but round-the-clock nonmedical custodial care in the home. Our staff does the shopping for people, then goes into their homes to help with meals and personal care. I had no experience in health care, so I went to school and learned about it." **Jean—an Entrepreneur**

She describes herself as a demanding person, someone who likes to be in control and who encourages her staff to work hard and be very good. Jean models this behavior daily with her own tough schedule, despite the progression of her multiple sclerosis. Jean's creativity, spirit, and drive have helped her overcome all obstacles, from societal constraints to physical disabilities. She describes herself as an entrepreneur who is driven, single-minded, success oriented, and hardworking. She says that "being an entrepreneur is a state of mind." Throughout her life, Jean has displayed strength and courage by charting her own course. She continues to do that today by operating a highly successful business despite the limitations of being confined to a wheelchair. She has consistently found ways to work around her problems. Jean states that her ability to be creative and believe in herself has enabled her to deal with many situations throughout her life.

> "I was very independent, even as a young child. If I didn't like someone, I would not play with them or eat lunch with them. If I didn't like what my friends were doing at any given time, I would just leave. I never let someone else's will or needs override my own." **Nancy—an Entrepreneur**

Nancy is a forty-nine-year-old hospital administrator. She is the eldest of three children in a middle-class urban family. Both of her parents worked and shared responsibilities at home. Nancy was an intelligent, observant child who did well in school. She was also strong willed and believed in herself from a very early age.

Everyone in Nancy's family was expected to help with the household chores. Her parents exemplified equality with regard to work and were constantly engaged in cross-gender tasks both inside and outside the home. For example, Nancy's mother often handled the painting and paperhanging while her father helped out with the cooking and laundry. Nancy helped with everything and soon realized she could do anything if she put her mind to it.

She has worked her way up through the ranks to the administrative position she holds today. She works hard and brings a creative and innovative style to the issues that must be handled by her department. The obstacles created by her superiors often frustrate her.

> "I won't let anything stop me. I will find a way to get around anything that interferes with the goals I have set. If there's an obstacle, I will move it." **Nancy—an Entrepreneur**

Nancy has worked hard to share with her coworkers her vision for the operation of her department. In so doing, she has created a department where her coworkers agree with her perspective and regard the proper functioning of the department as beneficial to themselves as well as to the hospital. Nancy's frustration and impatience kicks in when she is dealing with others who are less motivated to devote their energies to the successful completion of whatever project is under way. She also dislikes the competitive atmosphere that is sometimes fostered by upper management. She states: "My competition is myself, doing the best I can."

Nancy is a firm believer in creating good working relationships with others. She manages her department with an open-door policy that gives all coworkers the opportunity to voice their concerns and opinions. She runs her department as if it were her own small business within the larger setting of the hospital. But she always remains focused on finding a way to work with others in order to ensure the success of her projects and of the department as a whole. Nancy exemplifies the characteristics of the Entrepreneur within the setting of a larger company.

The Relationship Between Self-Concept and Behavior

Both Jean and Nancy have many traits in common as Entrepreneurs although Jean is self-employed and Nancy works for a large organization. Both are hardworking, highly motivated, and driven to be as good as they can be in their chosen endeavors. Both also value good working relationships and seek to attract others through their enthusiasm. Jean and Nancy have a great deal of confidence in themselves, which their parents inculcated in them when they were children, and this self-confidence has grown stronger over the years.

For both Jean and Nancy, their behavior in the workplace is a result of their earlier experiences and the ideas they had about themselves as children and now have as adults. For the most part, both women are relatively happy with the way they are handling their lives. However, there are times when their workaholic tendencies seem to dominate them. At those times, they may decide they would like to create a more balanced approach in their work style. To do this, they first have to become aware of the thoughts that maintain their current mode of behavior.

If you recognize some aspects of the Entrepreneur in your behavior and would like to make some changes of your own, we encourage you to use the following Work Role Exercise. The purpose of this exercise is threefold: (1) to identify the thoughts that maintain the role; (2) to change your thinking, which will then change your behavior; and (3) to create a plan for changing your behavior.

Entrepreneur Work Role Exercise

1. **What thoughts do you have about yourself that maintain the role of the Entrepreneur?**

   _____

   _____

2. **What evidence supports these thoughts?**

   _____

   _____

3. **What evidence disputes these thoughts?**

    _____

    _____

4. **What alternative behavior(s) would you like to exhibit?**

    _____

    _____

5. **What steps must you take in the short term (3–6 months) to progress toward this new behavior?**

    Step 1 _____

    Step 2 _____

    Step 3 _____

6. **What steps must you take in the long term (1–3 years) to progress toward this new behavior?**

    Step 1 _____

    Step 2 _____

    Step 3 _____

7. **What thoughts may interfere with your taking these steps?**

    _____

    _____

8. **What would you tell a friend who shared these concerns with you? Write down this alternative perspective and use it to motivate yourself to start changing your behavior.**

    _____

    _____

•　•　•

Conclusion

One major trap for the Entrepreneur is the possibility of isolating herself or of working with minimal help, which may significantly hamper her efforts to complete her project. This potential problem is due to the frustration and impatience the Entrepreneur feels and clearly shows when she's working with people who, she believes, either do not understand what she is trying to accomplish or do not share her belief in the project. The Entrepreneur may benefit from showing increased tolerance for those who do not share her vision. Changing our behavior requires that we first become aware of it. For most of us, our behavior is so automatic that we are not even aware of what we are doing. You can implement change by completing the exercises in this chapter and by identifying the behaviors you would like to stop, start, and continue.

THE ENTREPRENEUR: A PLAN OF ACTION

Stop	Being impatient with others who may not share your drive, vision, and goals
Start	Including others in your vision by presenting it more patiently and in a more understandable fashion
	Working to encourage others to become committed to the project by helping them find something personally meaningful in it
Continue	Building strong relationships with colleagues, customers, vendors, and other contacts
	Being an innovative risk taker
	Maintaining your spirit and individuality
	Being highly motivated and enthusiastic about the work
	Believing in the power of your ideas
	Being creative
	Being a good worker
	Being optimistic

For the Entrepreneur, work is more than a job; it is a way of life. It is her hobby, her passion, and her identity. She is consumed by her work, constantly thinking, creating, and planning future projects. Her enthusiasm is infectious, for when she speaks of her work, she comes alive. It is who she is and what she is all about. One of the most significant aspects of the role of the Entrepreneur is her belief in the power of her ideas, which contributes greatly to her success. It enables her to maintain an optimistic outlook regardless of the questioning and doubts of others. Even when faced with setbacks and negativity from others, her vision remains strong and clear, and she is able to continue working toward her goal. The undeterred perseverance and creativity of the Entrepreneur contribute to her winning role for success.

8 COMPARING AND COMBINING ROLES

Isn't there a little bit of each of these roles in every one of us? The short answer is "yes"; most of us can identify with different characteristics from these six roles. Most of us begin our professional lives by playing one role. As time goes by and we gain more work experience, take on more responsibilities, and receive promotions, our style changes, and we exhibit the characteristics of other roles. So if you see yourself as more eclectic, or a combination of a few of the roles, you are not alone. We change and grow as we learn more about ourselves and accumulate experience. Now let's take a look at the connections between the various roles.

COMPARE THE ROLES: GOALS

Pleaser	Maverick	Entrepreneur	Peacekeeper	Caregiver	Survivor
• To be accepted • To be liked by others • To avoid conflict	• To live life on her own terms • To maintain her independence despite societal pressures to conform	• To achieve and be successful by identifying a need and creatively filling it	• To avoid conflict at home and at work • To maintain emotional connections with the people in her life	• To take care of everyone around her • To develop a sense of closeness with the people in her life in order to feel worthy	• To avoid conflict • To feel worthy • To adapt to a variety of situations

The Pleaser, the Peacekeeper, the Caregiver, and the Survivor pursue similar goals. They want to be liked and accepted by others. In addition, the Caregiver, the Survivor, and the Pleaser seek external validation to make them feel worthy. Another characteristic shared by the Peacekeeper, the Survivor, and the Pleaser is the desire to avoid conflict. They base their workplace behavior on the way others feel about them and the external validation they receive.

The goals of the Maverick and the Entrepreneur differ from the other four. The Maverick wants to live life on her own terms and maintain her independence. The Entrepreneur's goal is to achieve and be successful. Although they do share certain characteristics, their behavior in the workplace differs. The Maverick cares more about doing things her way and will sometimes sacrifice the success of a project to preserve her independence, whereas the Entrepreneur wants to be successful and devotes all of her energies to that end. The women who assume these two roles maintain a strong sense of self and are motivated by internal factors, not the need for external validation.

Role Characteristics

The characteristics of the Pleaser, the Peacekeeper, the Caregiver, and the Survivor illustrate women's need to maintain connection with the people around them. These roles describe individuals who are focused on others. They look outside of themselves for cues on how to behave. These women typically are easy to work with, will take on additional responsibility without question, and will frequently refrain from expressing their opinions in the interest of maintaining harmony with their coworkers. These individuals keep the peace in the office by supporting others. They work hard to make sure that jobs are completed on time and in an efficient manner. They generally are liked by most of their colleagues. They create a pleasant working atmosphere and are often considered important and valued members of the team.

The Maverick and the Entrepreneur are less concerned about being liked and accepted by others. The Maverick cares most about charting her own course and remaining unconstrained by company standards and existing procedures. Her independence is often interpreted as rebellious and inflexible. Those who work directly with the Maverick and share her perspective feel valued and supported by her. Those who do not work with her see her as a difficult person. The Entrepreneur concentrates on developing new ideas and finding creative ways of implementing them. She is less concerned about the way she is seen by coworkers because she does not seek validation from anyone. It can be frustrating to work with an Entrepreneur because she is often so consumed with her own thought processes that she has little time or attention left over to provide direction to others. However, her coworkers don't necessarily feel it is difficult to work with her, just that she operates at a fast pace.

COMPARE THE ROLES: PERSONAL CHARACTERISTICS

Pleaser	Maverick	Entrepreneur	Peacekeeper	Caregiver	Survivor
• Respectful	• Independent	• Risk taker	• Keeps the peace	• Overly responsible	• Believes she has no control over her life
• Obedient	• Rebellious	• Develops new ideas	• Avoids conflict	• Problem solver	• Reactive
• Cooperative	• Inflexible	• Enthusiastic	• Stabilizing force in the office	• Concern for others	• Adaptive
• Does not develop or express her own thoughts and opinions	• Strong	• Hard-working		• Selfless	
	• Competent	• Self-motivated			

COMPARE THE ROLES: **STRENGTHS**

Pleaser	Maverick	Entrepreneur	Peacekeeper	Caregiver	Survivor
• Gets along well with others	• Sensitive	• Creative	• Sensitive	• Cares about others	• Strong
• Good listener	• Independent	• Enthusiastic	• Good listener	• Reliable	• Perseveres
• Adaptable	• Self-assured	• Risk taker	• Good mediator	• Dependable	• Cares about others
• Develops positive relationships	• Risk taker	• Industrious	• Adaptable	• Problem solver	• Dependable
• Cooperative	• Creative	• Self-reliant	• Team builder	• Good listener	• Team player
• Hard-working	• Problem solver	• Innovative	• Hard-working	• Hard-working	• Agreeable
	• Hard-working	• Confident	• Politically savvy		• Responsible
		• Hard-working			• Adaptable
					• Hard-working

Role Strengths

The women who represent these roles all work hard; what varies is their motivation. The Pleaser and the Peacekeeper expend their efforts in order to be liked and to avoid conflict. The Caregiver and the Survivor are seeking external validation to make them feel accepted and valued. The strengths of these four—the Pleaser, the Peacekeeper, the Caregiver, and the Survivor—contribute to the development of strong working relationships. Since their focus is on other people and they are concerned mostly with creating a harmonious environment, these roles function well together. Yet, in our experience, we have found that many of the women who occupy these four roles are unaware of their strengths, even though they use them regularly. When people do not recognize the things they do well, they concentrate on what they perceive to be their weaknesses, which often leads to poor self-image, low self-esteem, and possibly depression and anxiety. This skewed focus inhibits their ability to promote themselves and achieve professional success.

The Maverick and the Entrepreneur work hard because of their internal motivation and drive to succeed. They do not look outside of themselves for encouragement or validation. Instead, their self-confidence makes them innovative

COMPARE THE ROLES: **WEAKNESSES**

Pleaser	Maverick	Entrepreneur	Peacekeeper	Caregiver	Survivor
• Reluctant to take risks • Denies own needs • Lacks individuality • Overextends herself • Unwilling to set limits • Insecure • Allows others to take advantage of her	• Inflexible • Has difficulty working with others • Impatient • Not a team player • Has difficulty adapting to new environments • Has difficulty with authority figures • Not open to alternative opinions	• Impatient • Intolerant of the weaknesses of others • Has difficulty taking direction from others • Needs to be in control • Has difficulty working in structured environments	• Extremely sensitive to environment • Poor conflict management skills • Avoids risk • Hesitates to speak up for herself	• Feels overly responsible for others • Unable to set limits • Opinionated • At risk of burnout • Needs to be in control • Selfless	• Vulnerable • Takes everything personally • Reactive • Relinquishes control of her own life • No sense of self • Fear of the unknown • Fear of failure • Holds on to negative beliefs about herself

risk takers. These women typically are aware of their strengths and use them on a daily basis, which contributes significantly to their professional success.

Role Weaknesses

The weaknesses of the Pleaser, the Peacekeeper, the Caregiver, and the Survivor inhibit their personal and professional growth and development. To be successful, one must have a sense of oneself and the ability to maximize strengths and minimize weaknesses. The women who take on the roles of the Pleaser, the Peacekeeper, the Caregiver, and the Survivor do not bring a sense of themselves to their jobs—they are either unaware of their strengths or tend to dismiss them, and they magnify their weaknesses and allow them to define their identities and behavior. In addition, instead of applying their energies to their own careers, they spend it on meeting the needs of others.

The Maverick and the Entrepreneur are not affected as drastically by their weaknesses, which may lead to difficulty in creating good working relationships but otherwise are not as significant. Their strengths and their belief in themselves offset their weaknesses.

SENSITIVITY TO ENVIRONMENT: **SENSITIVITIES**

	Pleaser	Maverick	Entrepreneur	Peacekeeper	Caregiver	Survivor
Sensitivity to Others	80% to 100%	0% to 20%	60% to 80%	80% to 100%	80% to 100%	80% to 100%
	High	Low	Mid-range	High	High	High
Sensitivity to Culture	80% to 100%	0% to 20%	60% to 80%	80% to 100%	80% to 100%	60% to 80%
	High	Low	Mid-range	High	High	Mid-range
Sensitivity to Self	0% to 20%	80% to 100%	80% to 100%	0% to 20%	0% to 20%	0% to 20%
	Low	High	High	Low	Low	Low

Role Sensitivities

As we have stated previously, the Pleaser, the Peacekeeper, the Caregiver, and the Survivor are continually looking to others to assure them that they are liked, accepted, and worthy. In the office, these women focus on how they affect their coworkers and the relationships they have with them. Given this tendency, they are very aware of their interactions and acutely aware of what their coworkers feel and think about them. With this in mind, it is understandable that they would score at the high end of the Sensitivity to Others scale. These women generally also receive high scores on the Sensitivity to Company Culture scale because they are so intent on maintaining harmonious working relationships and avoiding conflict. Because of the Survivor's insecurities and need for validation, her sensitivity to others is somewhat higher than her sensitivity to company culture, because her interactions with other people seem more real to her than an amorphous relationship with the company culture. The Pleaser, the Peacekeeper, the Caregiver, and the Survivor concentrate most of their energies on anticipating and meeting the needs of others, while giving little if any thought to themselves. As a result, their scores on the Sensitivity to Self scale are low.

The scores for the Maverick and the Entrepreneur on all three scales are in marked contrast to those of the Pleaser, the Peacekeeper, the Caregiver, and the Survivor. The Maverick and the Entrepreneur usually fall within the low range on the Sensitivity to Others and Sensitivity to Company Culture scales. They do not focus to such an extent on the needs and dictates of others. Because of their greater self-confidence, they are able to attain for themselves the validation they need. The Maverick and the Entrepreneur are usually internally driven and concentrate on accomplishing their objectives regardless of the feelings of others and the dictates of the company culture. Their score on the Sensitivity to Self scale is usually high.

COMPARE THE ROLES: **TRAPS**

Pleaser	Maverick	Entrepreneur	Peacekeeper	Caregiver	Survivor
• Allows others to take advantage of her • Takes on more than she can handle successfully	• Boxes herself in with her own inflexibility	• Isolates herself, which slows down project completion	• Represses her own view, which may undermine advancement	• Fulfills the needs of others at the expense of her own needs	• Has no awareness of her strengths • Has no energy for personal growth and development

Role Traps

The Pleaser, the Peacekeeper, the Caregiver, and the Survivor are all vulnerable to traps that arise from their tendency to disregard themselves in order to be available for others. This undermines their ability to know themselves and test their limits, to find out what they are capable of doing when they risk expressing their own thoughts and putting them into action. The Pleaser attempts to do everyone's bidding. Her inability to say "no" and set limits allows others to take advantage of her, thus reducing the time she has available for her own work. Eventually, the Pleaser begins to feel frustrated because her efforts are not advancing her career. When the Peacekeeper represses her views in order to avoid conflict, she is denying herself the opportunity to show others what she as an individual has to offer the company. While her efforts at peacekeeping are certainly an asset, she must be careful not to ignore herself in the process. The Caregiver and the Survivor are both so busy attending to the needs of others that they give little thought to themselves and what they want. Their lack of self-awareness inhibits their ability to advance within their respective companies.

Conversely, the traps for the Maverick and the Entrepreneur result from their extreme self-absorption. Their minimal concern for others is often detrimental to the creation of good working relationships, which often leads to a crucial lack of support for their projects. The bottom line is that all of these traps compromise the ability to develop and advance professionally.

Conclusion

In this chapter, we have tried to illustrate the similarities and differences among the six roles. Whether one role describes you completely or you see yourself as a combination of several roles, the question is, how do these various characteristics affect you in the workplace?

We have chosen to describe these roles by giving examples of workplace behaviors to help you identify your own characteristics as well as those of your coworkers. Greater understanding of how you function, and why, will enable you to identify problems you may be experiencing at work and recognize the behavior that may be contributing to those problems. You may also have identified traits exhibited by some of your coworkers. Perhaps this will explain why certain work relationships are better than others. Stop and think about it. Have you ever heard yourself talking about one person and saying how well you work together, how you both seem to be on the same page? Conversely, have you ever complained about how hard it is to work with another person who does not listen to what you have to say and always wants things done her way?

The purpose of our discussion is not to pigeonhole or label anyone but to provide information. Why is this information important? Because it may help you understand why you are having problems at work, or why you are not advancing as you hoped you would, or why you may not be getting along with coworkers. In addition, it may help you pinpoint what you are doing that has contributed to your success. Perhaps the following questions will provide you with more information about the role you assume.

Role Identification Questions

1. With which role do you identify most closely?

_____

_____

2. Which role characteristics do you believe you possess?

_____

_____

3. What are your strengths?

_____

_____

4. What are your weaknesses?

_____

_____

5. Where do you fall on the scales of sensitivity to others, to company culture, and to self?

_____

_____

6. What are your short-term goals (3–6 months), and what steps must you take to achieve them?

_____

_____

7. **What are your long-term goals (1–3 years), and what steps must you take to achieve them?**

_____

_____

• • •

Armed with this information, you are now faced with a choice: to continue with the same behavior if it is working for you, or to change whatever behavior is detrimental to you. In order to develop a winning role, you must focus on your strengths, change behaviors that are undermining your success, and chart your own course. In the following chapters, we will present suggestions and strategies for changing your thinking and your behavior.

PART TWO

CHANGING OUR ROLES
TO SUCCEED AT WORK

9 UNDERSTANDING ROLES IN THE WORKPLACE

Leadership, company culture, and communication are essential components of any organization. Women's behavior with respect to these components results from their images of themselves and the roles they assume in the workplace. In this chapter, we will discuss how these roles affect women with regard to leadership, company culture, and communication.

Most organizations are based on the masculine perspective that values autonomy and independence. This establishes an environment in which we as working women must struggle to achieve success. An environment that values autonomy and independence does not embrace or encourage employees who function best through connection and mutuality. Women's behavior is based on a belief system that values connection and mutuality. These behaviors have not been seen in a positive light by society in general, which interprets women's concern for mutuality and relationships as dependency and labels it a weakness.

The masculine behaviors of autonomy and separateness constitute the "right" path for the development of a strong, independent, successful adult, according to prevailing social standards. This perspective is also evident in the male-dominant hierarchical structure of the business world. The traditional structure values and rewards autonomy and separation as the building blocks of success. Given this traditional structure and perspective, how do we as women succeed in a culture that neither acknowledges nor values our contributions? This challenge faces each of us every time we walk through the doors of our workplaces. Before we can address this challenge, we must first recognize the strengths that we bring with us to our jobs.

Women entering the workforce have effected one of the most enormous organizational changes ever experienced, due to our unique skills in leadership and communication. As we mentioned previously, an increased level of connection and mutuality characterizes women's working style. Such differences are the foundation for new ways of working and thinking about how work gets done within an organization. There is no longer one right or prescribed way to think about leadership or communication. Rather, the door has been kicked wide open for other, less traditional approaches. With these nontraditional alternatives comes opportunity and the promise of possibility. In order to make the most of this opportunity, we need a better understanding of the elements of an organization, including leadership, company culture, and communication. While this awareness is important for both men and women, we believe it is of critical importance to women, who are now able to assume leadership roles in organizations that were previously dominated by men.

Leadership Characteristics

Leadership is vital because of its powerful influence on individual and group behavior. Management theorist Warren Bennis cites five common characteristics of leaders: a guiding vision; a passion for their profession or action plan; integrity, which includes self-knowledge and maturity; trust; and curiosity. He also states that successful leaders attract others by communicating their commitment to a project or goal in a way that's exciting to others (Bennis, 1988). Leaders communicate ideas across organizational boundaries and hierarchical levels. According to Bennis, a leader's success depends on trust, in the sense that members of an organization feel their leader is fair and consistent, not arbitrary. He explains that great leadership invests an organization with a sense of empowerment, which is apparent in four themes: members feel significant, learning and competence are considered important, members feel part of the organizational community, and work is exciting (Bennis, 1988).

Researchers have investigated and written extensively about gendered leadership, or what has come to be known as women's and men's respective styles of leadership. Some researchers favor the so-called women's leadership style in terms of managerial success. Others believe that the notion of gendered management styles is a fad, and that to really succeed as a leader or a manager, women need to adopt the characteristics and behavior typically associated with male management. Still others suggest that women are succeeding as leaders, not by learning male styles of leadership, but through their own skills, attitudes, and experiences as women (Rosener, 1990). With all of this debate, it's difficult to separate what is trendy from what is lasting. With this said, we would like to discuss perceived leadership characteristics among men and women, and which leadership traits and behaviors ultimately are seen as essential for current and future success.

There are many stereotypes of women as leaders. These stereotypes are based on assumptions about the female personality and have little to do with managerial style. We believe, however, that a woman's leadership style derives from who she is as an individual, not from her gender. It is important to note that not all individuals exhibit traits consistent with gender norms; that is, not all women in leadership positions are nurturing and not all men in leadership positions are authoritarian. Many female tendencies, however—such as listening, nurturing, caring, sharing, and strong interpersonal development skills—are now thought to be among the critical traits of great leaders. A leader achieves this status based on an individual set of traits, which typically develops over time through observation, experience, reading, and training.

Differences in Leadership Style

Men and women experience the world differently and bring these experiences to bear as leaders. One research study exploring effective management and leadership found that women were more effective managers and leaders than their male counterparts (Moskal, 1997). A study of more than nine hundred managers at companies such as Bank of America, Johnson & Johnson, Kinko's, Eastman Kodak, and General Electric found that women's effectiveness as managers, leaders, and teammates surpasses that of their male counterparts in twenty-eight of thirty-one managerial skill areas. The areas in which women outperformed men include resolving conflicts, producing higher-quality work, adapting to change, developing their own capabilities, and motivating and inspiring others.

Women also received higher scores in the category of communication, which includes articulating ideas, listening to others, keeping others informed, giving feedback on job performance, and communicating expectations (Moskal, 1997). The findings suggest that women are more likely to provide advice and guidance on how to complete a project and will clarify the expected outcomes with those who are doing the work. Men were less precise when articulating the guidelines or scope of a project. Men and women scored the same on one task—delegating authority. The category of managing self, which includes handling pressure, coping with frustrations, developing one's capabilities, and responding to feedback, was the most problematic category for women. Women tend to discuss their frustrations, sharing them with others, while men often view talking about one's problems as a weakness, whether it is a man or a woman who is engaging in the behavior. Men scored higher in handling pressure and coping with their own frustrations.

The findings in this study support traditional as well as nontraditional gender roles, abilities, and strengths. Interestingly, women in the study rated themselves lower than men in each skill area, confirming that women undervalue the abilities, knowledge, and skills they bring to the workplace.

In 1996, *The Economist* and Korn/Ferry International surveyed senior-level global executives in order to identify top traits in female and male managers. The traits listed are consistent with traditional conceptions of gender behavior. Female managerial traits include empathy, supportiveness, nurturing ability, interest in building relationships, and willingness to share. The managerial traits found in men include willingness to take risks, self-confidence, competitiveness, decisiveness, and directness (Wangensteen, 1997).

According to a five-year study of gender and leadership skills, women and their coworkers, both male and female, believe that women are significantly better managers than men (Pfaff, 1999). Female managers scored higher than their male counterparts in twenty skill areas, including communication, feedback, empowering other employees, decisiveness, and developing and setting standards.

This study looked at 2,482 managers at all levels from more than four hundred organizations in nineteen states. According to Pfaff, women have acquired non-traditional strengths in recent years, whereas men have not expanded their skills in a comparable way. Given the current interest in more supportive, collaborative, and cooperative ways of working, women are in a better position to meet this need. Specifically, the study reports that women's socialization has prepared them to facilitate group processes, motivate employees in positive ways, and develop the abilities of others. Furthermore, the study indicates that men rely on a more autocratic style of leadership that emphasizes individual accomplishment and competition.

Women value connection and inclusion, working together for a common goal. When the dominant culture directs them to adapt to a male style of working and leadership, they are being asked to turn their backs on their strengths and beliefs. In so doing, they significantly diminish their effectiveness and power. It's like trying to function with one hand tied behind your back. We cannot have an effective, diverse workforce if diversity is being sacrificed to preserve the belief system of the dominant culture. A closed or rigid culture not only stifles employees, it is also detrimental to the financial well-being and future of the company.

Leadership has been defined as relationship-based because leaders function in relation to others. It is interesting to note that the concepts of connection and relationship have traditionally been associated with women. The need to feel close to others is very much a part of a woman's identity and should not be categorized as a weakness or a deficiency (Stiver, 1991).

As women, we must first identify our innate strengths, which we often take for granted, and value them. We bring to leadership a focus on mutuality that empowers both parties and enables them to understand and respond to each other (Surrey, 1991). Beginning in childhood, relationships play an important part in our lives. Connection with others is the way we live and grow. Difficulty develops as women enter the workplace and are expected to function within the male-defined corporate culture. The concept of power within the workplace is frequently a troubling issue for many women, due in large measure to its present hierarchical and competitive structure. Women often envision power in terms of isolation; this is contrary to the ways in which most women choose to work and see themselves. Women can deal more effectively with the concept of power when they view it within the context of empowering relationships.

We as women have been reared with a unique gift, and our respect for connection can bring concern for others and the ability to empower others into the

OUACHITA TECHNICAL COLLEGE

> "I think of myself as someone who cares about providing a happy working environment. It's a rather selfish sort of thing. It's much easier for me when people are happy. I see myself as somebody who improves performance by helping people do what they need to do." **Jane—a Maverick**

workplace. When we allow ourselves to utilize the full range of our skills, we enhance our own success as well as that of our employers. As the business world becomes more diverse, there is a greater need for inclusive leadership. However, few women have been able to attain leadership status in many large companies because the dominant culture is still trying to maintain the status quo.

A 1990 study conducted by Judy Rosener found that women "encourage participation, share power and information, enhance other people's self-worth, and get others excited about their work." These abilities increase an individual's sense of power and importance. They create a win-win situation for both employer and employee.

When we talk about leaders, we are referring not only to managers, directors, senior executives, or those with formal leadership titles. We are talking about working in all capacities, at all levels, and about our ability to affect our coworkers and environment. Regardless of our jobs or positions, we are continually interacting with coworkers, and in so doing, we are utilizing leadership skills such as empowering, nurturing, communicating, supporting, and sharing information. These skills are intuitive for many women. They are consistent with the roles women have occupied throughout the ages. As women, we employ these skills in the many areas of our personal lives, and we now have the opportunity to bring them into the workplace.

> "A female boss is more willing to talk about you—who you are, your entire self, personally and professionally. Whether you are working with a boss or a colleague, a man will start to push you away as soon as you get a little too close." **Kate—a Survivor**

Effective leadership traits are not new to us as women. What is new is that the business world is slowly beginning to acknowledge the value of these skills in helping organizations to function more effectively. But while research and organizations are slowly beginning to recognize and value relationship skills in the workplace, many women do not. Many women are still convinced that the ability to develop and maintain relationships is not really a skill. In so doing, they devalue one of their major strengths in the workplace. If we want to feel valued in the workplace, we must first learn to value ourselves. The first step in seeing ourselves as effective members of any organization is becoming aware of our skills and abilities.

Leadership Style and the Six Roles

The Peacekeeper's leadership style is strong and embraces the people who work for her. She has the best interests of her colleagues at heart and will go to bat for them when necessary, as long as it does not cause conflict. Those who work for the Peacekeeper have strong feelings about her, which are generally very positive. Her subordinates view her as an influential leader within their department and within the larger organization. They look to their Peacekeeper boss as a role model; they feel they can learn from her use of interpersonal skills. She is seen as a mentor by many of her subordinates because she takes pride in developing others at work. She is a leader who strives to create future leaders by working within the corporate culture.

As a leader, the Pleaser is respectful of others, superiors and subordinates alike. She does not develop or express ideas of her own but rather follows the direction already set by others, preferring to conform to the expectations and decisions of the larger company. However, the Pleaser is a dependable leader who will take on additional responsibilities in order to please her superiors. At times, she will agree to do things she may not have the authority or ability to do. This creates problems with coworkers and her superiors. While her subordinates like her overall because she is

"My leadership style is to get people to interact as a team. I need to get them to think like a team because recruiting is a lonely field. Recruiters work by themselves in the marketplace. You're alone in your office, dealing with the marketplace. So my challenge as a leader is to take people who have that type of function and encourage them to interact as a group—otherwise, they will not be successful. I have to make them trust me." **Lisa—a Peacekeeper**

"My greatest strengths are my ability to get along with people and my willingness to acknowledge other people's contributions. I believe that when you acknowledge people for their good work, the result is an increase in productivity. I believe this makes me a good manager. I run my department differently from the rest of the company. My leadership style is marked by respect, trust, and caring. At times, this perspective is seen as weak by my colleagues." **Ilene—a Pleaser**

"My leadership style is very different from the larger organization's. It's more involved and hands-on. I think it's important to create a structure and a clear definition of what people are supposed to do. It's important for me to set a vision and manage people in a way that allows them to feel comfortable and realize their potential. I have very high standards." **Jane—a Maverick**

"My leadership style is collaborative. I think about the needs of others and their feelings when I'm asking them to do something. I think you get more out of people when you treat them as friends, nicely and respectfully. Hopefully they appreciate it and do what you want them or need them to do." **Rachel—a Caregiver**

"I don't think I'm very good at managing people. I have a hard time telling people when they haven't done something correctly. I try to keep it positive; I tell them I know they tried their best but maybe they could do the job a different way. Then I suggest an alternative. I find myself thinking, who am I to tell them if they are right or wrong?" **Kate—a Survivor**

agreeable and easygoing, they are sometimes frustrated by her behavior, specifically her inability to come up with new ideas and her hesitation about making decisions.

The Maverick's leadership style is characterized by doing things her way. She needs control over the work process and ensures it by recruiting people into her work group or department who share her values and vision. This type of focused hiring results in connection and loyalty. She is more concerned with her own needs and those of her work group than with the needs of the larger organization. She organizes her department by establishing a vision she feels comfortable with and ensuring that her vision is understood and respected by others.

The Caregiver's leadership style is characterized by her supportive nature. She takes every opportunity to acknowledge people for the work they have done and encourages them to move ahead to the tasks that remain. She is very attentive to the needs of her coworkers and puts a great deal of effort into creating an environment where everyone's needs can be met. The Caregiver focuses on building positive working relationships among her coworkers. Her emphasis on relationships supports an inclusive environment where everyone feels like a vital part of the team.

The Survivor's leadership style is characterized by her compliance and endurance. Regardless of the situation, the Survivor continues to do whatever she believes is expected of her in order to keep things running smoothly. She leads by encouraging others to fall into line and do their best without question. She is not a creative or innovative leader; instead, she adheres strictly to company policy and encourages compliance within her work group or department. The Survivor is a dependable and responsible individual who gets the most from those who work under her direction and, at the same time, gives the most to her superiors.

The Entrepreneur's leadership style is characterized by her strength and unwavering concentration on the project at hand. Like the Maverick, she is selective about the people she includes in her work group or department. By bringing together like-minded individuals who share her values and perspective, she creates a cohesive and dedicated group. She is a tireless worker who leads by example. Because she is self-motivated, she often assumes that others share her drive and determination. Therefore, she may not provide the kind of direction that results in successful completion of the project. This lack of direction is often frustrating for both the Entrepreneur and her coworkers.

> "I'm very demanding, and I am always in control. I understand the people who are working for me, what tasks I've assigned to whom, what their strengths are. I then align their strengths and skills appropriately and hold them accountable. I'm very up-front about what needs to be done, what my expectations are, and what my working style is. Some people may be a bit intimidated by it, but others find it refreshing."
>
> **Nancy—an Entrepreneur**

Identifying Your Leadership Style

The inherent strength of both the Maverick and the Entrepreneur is evident in their descriptions of their respective leadership styles. Likewise, the statements of the Peacekeeper, the Pleaser, the Caregiver, and the Survivor illustrate their tendency to be other-focused in their leadership styles. All of the women we interviewed try to create meaningful and positive relationships with their coworkers; however, their styles vary and are characteristic of their respective roles.

After reading over these six viewpoints on leadership style, do you think you have a good sense of your own style? Whether or not you are presently in a leadership position at work, take a few minutes to think through the following exercise. Its goal is to heighten your awareness of your own leadership style.

Leadership Style Exercise

1. **How would you describe your leadership style?**

   _____

   _____

2. **How would your subordinates and/or coworkers describe your leadership style?**

_____

_____

3. **Does a discrepancy exist between your perception and the perception of those with whom you work with regard to your leadership style? If so, explain.**

_____

_____

4. **What changes would you like to make to your leadership style?**

_____

_____

• • •

Leadership and the Support and Advisory Group

Leaders are often identified in individual terms because their traits are examined, their styles are described, and their results are measured (Stech 1983). While leaders may be studied in isolation, in reality, great leaders surround themselves with a significant support and advisory base. It is critical for all of us, leaders and nonleaders alike, to develop a strong support and advisory group (SAG). If you were a car running on empty, this is the group that would get you "filled up" again. This group serves as a reality check, to keep you from getting stuck in negative circular thinking that can lead to a feeling of being overwhelmed, which can then stifle or inhibit positive behaviors. Your individual SAG can help you identify your problems, encourage you to start thinking about how to solve them, and finally, help you come up with solutions. Your group has a real purpose: it gives you the opportunity to receive input from people you trust.

A base of support may consist of family members, close friends, coworkers, or former coworkers. Regardless of its makeup, this network is just as important, if not more important, as any other, because your group will strengthen you, evaluate your ideas, and allow you to express your emotions. It's also important to be a member of someone else's group. Are you there for the people who are there for you? You must realize that in order to maintain your SAG, you have to be an effective SAG member. Does this seem a bit unusual? A little out of the ordinary? Well, good. We want you to start, or hope you will be continuing, to think in terms of community. Even the most independent person needed someone else at some point to help her learn and grow.

Support and Advisory Group (SAG) Questions

1. **Do you have a support and advisory group (SAG)?**

    _____

2. **If so, who are the group members?**

    _____

3. **Who are your SAG members for personal issues and concerns?**

    _____

4. **Who are your SAG members for professional issues and concerns?**

    _____

5. **If you do not have a SAG, what gets in the way of having this group? What can you do about this?**

    _____

    _____

6. **Do you seek support and counsel from others and feel comfortable and secure that you have people to speak with about issues that arise?**

    _____

• • •

Organizational Culture

An organization's long and complex history eventually produces a mature culture. When organizations or groups initially form, there typically are dominant figures, or "founders," whose personal beliefs, values, and assumptions offer a visible and articulated model for the group's structure and manner of functioning (Schein, 1985). That culture then creates patterns of perception, thought, and feeling within each new generation and becomes predisposed to certain types of leadership. Through its culture, the mature group creates its own leaders. Schein (1985) describes this paradox by stating that "leaders create cultures, but cultures, in turn, create their next generation of leaders."

Culture encompasses the behavior patterns of an identified group of people and the commonality that exists in the group's ways of thinking, feeling, and acting (Brown, 1963). Elements of organizational culture include, but are not limited to, stories of organizational life, organizational values, and heroes, such as role models, rituals, and language—all of which characterize work life. Culture can be created in two ways: first, through the formation of norms and beliefs that result from members' responses to critical events; and second, the internalization of leaders' values and assumptions by group members (Schein, 1990).

It is increasingly critical for women to learn about the culture of the organization for which they work. While most workplaces are changing and becoming more diverse, corporate cultures historically have been developed and controlled by white men (Ruderman, Ohlott, and Kram, 1995). As a result, women may have a difficult time understanding and functioning within a culture whose norms were designed by and for men. This doesn't mean that women are unable to learn the culture; it just may be harder for them to understand and exhibit the behaviors required to reach the executive suite. Women learn about their company culture by informal means, as participants and as observers of coworkers and senior leaders.

Corporate Culture and the Six Roles

"One of the things I can say about my career is that I've been blissfully unaware until recently of the effects of the culture on the people who work in it. I have always sort of shoved aside all of my instincts about whether or not something was inappropriate if I thought it gave me a chance to fulfill my potential." **Jane—a Maverick**

The Peacekeeper is a strong proponent of and believer in the corporate culture of her employer. She is not one to bend or liberally interpret the rules and policies of the organization. The Peacekeeper is similar to the Caregiver, the Pleaser, and the Survivor in her adherence to the company culture. Each of those four roles is concerned about avoiding conflict and remaining within the established parameters of the organization. Alternatively, the Maverick and the Entrepreneur are less concerned about working within the confines of the corporate culture. They are both interested in their own needs and goals, regardless of whether or not their behavior fits the requirements of the corporate culture.

Every company has a culture, and the departments, divisions, and business units within the larger company have subcultures that can be quite different from the larger corporate culture.

Through learning about the culture, we become more invested in the organization. We begin to understand what we need to do at work in order to reach our goals. We define success within the organization, determine whether it is something to which we aspire, then function accordingly. In large part, learning about your company's culture is subconscious and experiential, which means that with each passing day, you acquire more knowledge and become more invested in the culture. Notice your own work environment. When you walk into your office building in the morning, how comfortable do you feel? What is the tone of the office? What is the decor like? What is posted on the walls? How do people speak to one another? How do things really get done? What does it feel like to be at work? That, in a nutshell, is organizational culture, and whether we intend to or not, we become a part of it. The following questions should help you clarify your thoughts about your company culture.

"I crafted the equivalent of a separate business unit, which was very important to me. I feel as though I'm in a small business unit that's been developed according to my vision, and the people in it fit my cultural requirements." **Nancy—an Entrepreneur**

"Need to learn about the culture to fit in. You need to learn and observe. How do people communicate here? How do leaders talk to each other? How do staff members talk to each other? How do leaders talk to the staff? I always tell people when they join the company to watch how I respond, how I write that memo, then they'll pick up how we talk to each other here." **Lisa—a Peacekeeper**

Organizational Culture Questions

1. **Are you able to articulate the culture of your organization and of your division, business unit, work group, or department?**

_____

_____

2. **Are you comfortable in the culture? If so, can you pinpoint the elements that make you feel that way?**

_____

_____

3. **If you are not comfortable, what are the factors that contribute to your discomfort?**

_____

_____

4. **Are you able to change your work environment so that you are comfortable and productive within the existing culture?**

_____

_____

5. **Describe your ideal corporate culture (one in which you would feel comfortable being yourself and being productive).**

_____

_____

● ● ●

Women and Communication

Communication is the fabric we use to weave our lives. We communicate to others as others communicate to us. We engage in verbal and nonverbal modes of communication throughout our young lives and bring that interactive style to the various organizations to which we belong, such as the family organization, the friends organization, and the formal work setting. We exercise our communication style and skills in the same way that we work out our muscles. We stretch them, strengthen them, and continue to develop them as we collect new experiences and learning.

For women, communication equals connection with other people, in other words, discovering what we have in common and creating networks of intimacy (Tannen, 1994). Catching up with a friend or a coworker, getting your point across, hearing other people's thoughts or being heard by others, these are all opportunities for increased connection and understanding—for women, that is. Communication for women reflects the way we see ourselves, as individuals within a community. We use communication to maintain connection, create closeness, and give and receive support. Women bring unique communication skills to the workplace, as they are more cooperative, participative, and affiliative than the directive style displayed by men (Grant, 1988).

For men, a conversation is a negotiation in which they try to achieve status and maintain their independence (Tannen, 1994). Communication between men is a competition of power and will. The goal is to emerge the obvious winner and avoid being viewed as weak (Tannen, 1994). For most men, communication represents a means to an end and usually takes the form of information gathering. Once the information is gathered, the conversation is over.

These varying styles set up an imbalance of power. An individual who uses a directive style of communication may perceive someone who utilizes a participative style as weak, nonassertive, and short on knowledge and conviction. This person may therefore appear less credible and will not be able to claim as much attention as the individual with the directive style of communication. Sometimes a person with a directive style can be very intimidating to others. However, an authoritative tone doesn't necessarily guarantee correctness or the possession of superior knowledge. Similarly, someone with a participative style who creates a sense of community during the decision-making process should not be seen as weak, unintelligent, or irresolute. While this approach requires more time to reach a consensus or produce a decision, it is inclusive in nature and thus results in shared focus and greater commitment from team members.

It is important to remember that these differing communication patterns are yet another example of the gender difference we discussed earlier: men are autonomous, women are affiliative. The crucial question is, how can the directive approach coexist in the workplace with the participative approach? Both styles have merit and are necessary in different situations. We must be careful not to value or condemn one style over the other. It is imperative to be aware of this difference in communication patterns and to regard it as just that, a difference to be worked out, not a weapon to be used in a power struggle.

Communication Style and the Six Roles

The communication style of each of the six roles clearly illustrates personality—some are direct, some are tentative, and others are confident about the messages they transmit. Communication style shows how we feel about ourselves and how we wish to be treated. The Peacekeeper's communication style is team focused. She is most concerned about creating consensus, hearing people out, and having them listen to her. The Peacekeeper will reach the final decision by communicating her position and persuading others to agree.

> "People who work for me say I'm different. I'm much more present for my staff. I think I'm present for my staff more than any of the other leaders I've worked with. I think I'm an arbitrator." **Lisa—a Peacekeeper**

The Pleaser's communication style is agreeable. Her goal is to please others, and in keeping with this goal, the Pleaser enjoys delivering messages that she feels her audience wants to hear. She communicates messages crafted by others in order to conform to other people's expectations of her. The Pleaser worries that she will say the wrong thing and upset those who share her work environment. She has strong listening skills and is very attentive to the needs of others.

> "When I'm speaking with others, I'm always attentive, trying very hard to hear what their needs are. I think people want to feel validated, and I try to give them that." **Ilene—a Pleaser**

The Maverick's communication style is direct. She is clear about what she wants to say and the ideas she needs to get across. She is less concerned about her style of communicating with others or what they need in this regard; her primary interest is to make her position known. The Maverick's communication style is generally well received within her own group, but this is not necessarily true of the larger organization. There, she typically is misunderstood and considered too direct and insensitive to corporate culture and policies.

> "My communication style is somewhat more direct, more open. I tend to operate on the premise that 'what you see is what you get.' I don't mask my feelings and thoughts like they do in the rest of the organization. In most business environments where men are predominant, I think you have much less openness and candor. I'm lucky that I work much of the time for organizations that are run by women or have a lot of women in them." **Jane—a Maverick**

The Caregiver's communication style is participative. She is most interested in making sure that others feel she has heard what they have to say and that she is available to them. The Caregiver appreciates this style of communication in return. When she does not receive it, she feels that she is being pushed to the side and no one hears her or cares about her. People generally feel comfortable speaking with the Caregiver because of her interest and concern. She is a strong communicator who is attuned to the thoughts, concerns, and needs of her coworkers.

"I'm more into explaining things one-on-one, more so than others are. My communication style is less aggressive than that of the management of my company."
Rachel—a Caregiver

The Survivor's communication style is subdued. She prefers speaking individually with a single person. She is extremely uncomfortable when speaking in front of more than one person because she feels she has little to offer and is unimportant. The Survivor's low self-esteem has a significant impact on her ability and willingness to speak with others.

"My communication style is not very good. I'm not a very good speaker. I don't feel that I could speak in front of a group. I feel as though what I have to say is not that important. " **Kate—a Survivor**

The Entrepreneur's communication style is marked by her direct, no-nonsense approach. The purpose of her communication is to get results: to ensure that her coworkers have a clear understanding of what is expected and consequently will follow through. The Entrepreneur is a strong, confident person, and this is evident in her mode of communication. At times, others may interpret this strong, direct style as intimidating or rude; however, that is not the Entrepreneur's intention.

"My communication style is very direct. I have a very clear idea of what needs to be done, and I communicate it succinctly. It may appear to some people that I can be somewhat insulting or disrespectful. My style is very honest and very sincere, but it can be a little in-your-face. I don't mind that."
Nancy—an Entrepreneur

Individual and Organizational Communication Styles

Clearly, the interviewees have spent time reflecting on their styles and changing and reshaping them as the situation required. Perhaps they picked up cues in their environments through observing others, or attending a training class, or receiving coaching feedback on their communication skills. Regardless of the reasons, our style, while relatively stable, evolves over time. It is reshaped and assumes different characteristics as we change and grow. Like our environment, we are not static. We are dynamic, flexible beings.

Communication within organizations conveys information about individual roles, organizational goals, and status. Communication, however, can only be effective if it is received and understood by the intended audience. Communication has the power to influence values and beliefs when it is delivered in a way that fosters belief and deepens trust. Organizational communication takes a variety of forms. One-on-one communication, small-group communication, and large-group verbal, nonverbal, and written communication are all vehicles by which people are brought together, physically and emotionally. To get people to share a common vision or goal, to sort through an issue or solve a problem, these are all critical goals of organizational communication.

Use the following exercise to examine and compare your communication style and the communication style of your company.

Communication Exercise

1. Describe your communication style.

_____

_____

2. Describe your organization's communication style.

_____

_____

3. Do any discrepancies exist between your style and that of the organization?

_____

_____

4. Are there aspects of your communication style that you feel you need to address or change?

_____

_____

• • •

Women are faced with a challenge in the workplace. They must integrate their complete identities and unique qualities into the existing organizational structure and culture. Each woman brings with her different behaviors that are representative of her role and thus exhibits varied leadership and communication styles. Her role also determines her acceptance into the corporate culture. In the following chapters, we will present cognitive and behavioral strategies that you can use to increase your success at work.

10 CHANGING THE WAY WE THINK

After reviewing the various roles and determining the characteristics that best describe you, you need to decide whether these behaviors are helping or hindering you at work. If they are helpful, you should continue these behaviors and ask yourself what more you can do to enhance your success. For example, although Entrepreneurs have many skills, they sometimes have difficulty communicating their vision and strategy to their coworkers. In this instance, the Entrepreneur would benefit from working on her communication skills. If, on the other hand, you find that your behaviors are hindering you at work, then you need to determine what changes to make.

This course of action would be helpful for the Survivor, who has not developed her own identity and resigns herself to her situation. She would benefit from becoming aware of the self-concepts that contribute to her reactive behavior.

No matter which role you've assumed, the option for change exists. Change is the process of identifying the behaviors or characteristics you feel are not working for you and altering them in order to facilitate your success. In the following chapters, we will view change from cognitive and behavioral perspectives. We will present tools that can help you make those changes you consider necessary to adapt successfully to your work environment.

A Cognitive Therapy Approach to Change

Throughout this book, our aim has been to inform you about the process of women's development and the forces that affect it. We have discussed how the messages we receive from family and society contribute to the formation of our beliefs about ourselves and the roles we assume. Armed with this information, you now have the opportunity to evaluate the effectiveness of your role in your life. Very simply put, has this type of behavior worked for you? If the answer is "yes," then how has it worked? What are the benefits of living your life in this role? If the answer is "no," then why hasn't it worked? What has been the cost of living your life in this role? Use the chart on page 125 to evaluate the benefits and costs of your role.

After you complete the chart, you will be in a position to make an informed decision regarding what path to take at this point in your life. You may choose to continue on your present path, or you may choose to change the way you see yourself and your way of functioning.

The process of making choices begins in childhood, and decisions are often made based on familial or societal expectations. When you were growing up, you may have tried to figure out which behaviors helped you fit in and cope with the expectations of family and society. At that time, you had limited information about yourself and the world around you, and this may have narrowed your choices. As an adult, you have more freedom and more options. Your experiences in life have provided you with more information about yourself and the world in which you live. Now you have the opportunity to change your way of functioning. There is no reason to continue with old behaviors if they are no longer working for you, particularly if they are not meeting the needs of the woman you are today.

Benefits and Costs of Your Role

	Benefits	**Costs**
Role as Child	_____	_____
	_____	_____

	Benefits	**Costs**
Role as Adult	_____	_____
	_____	_____

	Benefits	**Costs**
Role in Workplace	_____	_____
	_____	_____

• • •

We like to refer to this as our "then and now" theory. Then, as a child, you were under more pressure to do what was expected of you because you needed to receive care, love, acceptance, and approval for being a good little girl. Now, as an adult woman, you can take care of yourself. You can choose to break free of the old constraints and redefine yourself. The opportunity is yours.

It is important to realize that it is never too late to change. We are not suggesting that you change who you are; we are suggesting that you change your perception of yourself. For in order to change your behavior, you must first change the way you think. We are encouraging you to recognize your strengths, value who you are, and bring your complete self to everything you do, personally and professionally. Throughout this book, we have asked you to complete exercises designed to increase your awareness of the perceptions you have about yourself and the various issues that affect you. These exercises are based on the principles of Cognitive Therapy. Once you achieve this heightened awareness, you will be able to analyze the validity of your thinking and develop alternative viewpoints. This shift in thinking will then lead to a change in behavior in all areas of your life.

Forming Beliefs About Ourselves

From the time we are born, we begin receiving information about ourselves from everyone around us. As babies, we cry in order to get our needs met. When someone attends to those needs, we are comforted. The message comes across that we are valued, loved, and surrounded by trustworthy people who will take care of us. Unmet needs send negative messages that lay the foundation for a different set of beliefs, such as distrust and the conviction that we are unlovable and unworthy.

As we grow, we continue to receive verbal and nonverbal messages from our parents, siblings, and extended family about how cute we are, how smart we are, and how difficult or easy it is to care for us. We begin to be defined and identified by our behavior and our impact upon others. How others treat us and what they tell us about ourselves become our sources of information about ourselves. We take in all of this information and begin to develop beliefs about ourselves. These different beliefs then form what we have come to refer to as our self-concept. This is an interesting choice of words because the term *self-concept* refers to an individual's perception of herself; however, in reality, this image of ourselves is a function of how others see us. It is the reflection we see in the eyes of others.

When we begin attending school, our world expands, and more messages begin rolling in from teachers, friends, and society at large. There is a reciprocal interaction, or feedback loop, between the messages we hear, the beliefs we form about ourselves, and our behavior.

The quotes of Peg, a Survivor, and Lisa, a Peacekeeper, illustrate how the feedback loop operates. Suppose you are continually criticized and corrected as a child. You may begin to think that nothing you do is right and that you are not good enough. You may then develop feelings of insecurity and behave in a tentative manner or perhaps withdraw. The more you function in a tentative, insecure fashion, the more you are criticized and the worse you feel about yourself.

On the other hand, suppose you are continually praised as a child. These messages may contribute to your belief that you are a competent and capable individual. This would lead to feelings of confidence and a readiness to meet challenges and deal with problems. The more successful you are in

"My mother always told me that I would never amount to anything. I thought that I was dumb. From childhood on, I was shy, very quiet, and had very low self-esteem. Because I felt so insecure, I allowed others to push me around. It wasn't until I was on my own, a divorced mother of two, that I began to recognize my strengths and my intelligence. I started to express myself. I started to discover who I was and to become my own person." Peg—a Survivor

your endeavors, the more you are praised, and the better you feel about yourself.

Our beliefs about ourselves are integral to our behavior and our interactions with others. You could think of them as statements that have been recorded on a tape, and this tape is always on as you go through life. The experiences you had and the messages you received while you were growing up created this tape. For people with low self-esteem, the tape has a greater number of negative statements than positive ones. Likewise, for individuals with high self-esteem, the tape has a much greater percentage of positive statements. The tape plays at very low volume, almost muted, but you can still hear it, guiding and directing you at every turn. Certain situations seem to push the volume-control button, and the tape gets louder, almost screaming all the negative thoughts it has recorded so that you can't ignore them. These thoughts affect your behavior. You could also think of these situations as trigger situations, since they activate a flow of negative thoughts about yourself. It is important to note that the tape with these messages does not have to be permanent, no matter how long it has been in existence.

> "The one thing both my parents taught me, which has done more for me than anything else in my life, was that no matter where I went, I was always going to be faced with people who were prettier than me, taller than me, richer than me, more powerful than me. You are always going to be faced with someone like that. But no one would ever be better than me." **Lisa—a Peacekeeper**

Changing the Beliefs

Like a tape recorder, your brain can fast-forward, rewind, and, most important, record. You have the option of recording over old messages that have been running through your head. You can begin by identifying these thoughts. What are you telling yourself? Next, writing these thoughts down will provide a little emotional distance and give you a chance to evaluate their accuracy. What evidence have you gathered from your experiences that either supports or disputes these thoughts? Going through this process will allow you to find another way of looking at the situation. Sometimes it helps to stop and think about what you would tell your best friend if she had this problem. The goal of this process is to become your own best friend.

The process we have just described is called Cognitive Therapy and was developed by Dr. Aaron Beck. Cognitive Therapy is based on the assumption that our way of thinking affects our feelings and behavior (Beck, 1976). Throughout this book, there are examples of women's belief systems and the impact their beliefs have had on their behavior, particularly at work. There are also exercises for you to complete that should help you identify your beliefs about yourself, how these beliefs are affecting your professional life, and what you can do to change them. But before we can change our beliefs, we need to be aware of how we view ourselves.

The Impact of Negative Beliefs at Work

"As a child, I recall feeling insecure about my skills and abilities. My confidence plummeted through the years because of my poor grades in school. The difficulties I experienced in school spread to other areas of my life. I was afraid to speak up in class, with friends, and at home. As an adult at work, I find I don't like to take risks. When something does not go as planned in my department, I immediately attribute the problem to something I did wrong, then shut down in order to protect myself." **Kate—a Survivor**

"My parents always told me that I was smart, had many talents, and would succeed in anything if I put my mind to it. So no matter what kind of boardrooms I've had to walk into, no matter what kind of senior leadership meetings I've participated in, no matter what anyone says to me, I've always held onto that belief. A senior executive may have more power but will never be better than me. I've never lost that piece of confidence."

Lisa—a Peacekeeper

In order to succeed professionally, women must be confident and secure in their abilities. Women who have negative beliefs about themselves are often hesitant and insecure at work. Their negative beliefs interfere with their ability to work at their optimum levels.

On the other hand, women with positive beliefs are very comfortable with their ability to verbalize their opinions, thoughts, and feelings at work. These women received positive messages about themselves when they were growing up, understand how the game of work is played, and put themselves and their beliefs on the line.

Our beliefs about ourselves can facilitate or sabotage our ability to adapt. Those of us who have a larger number of positive beliefs may be able to take an objective look at the situation and apply our strengths to the demands of the job. Those of us who have a negative belief system will tend to see the demands of the job as evidence of our lack of skills. Negative thinking interferes with your ability to adapt and solve problems. A useful tool for dealing with negative thinking is the Thoughts Identification and Response Exercise. This exercise will heighten your awareness of the impact of your negative thinking and provide you with a tool for changing your thoughts and behavior.

We encourage you to write out the answers to each of these questions. Writing down your thoughts will give you the distance you need to analyze them more objectively, which will enable you to develop a more rational view of the situation. The more frequently you engage in this process, the more natural it will become to you, and you will no longer need to write it out. The ultimate goal of this process is to avoid immediate negative thoughts and go directly to a more rational, balanced perspective that takes all the evidence into consideration. Whenever you feel yourself becoming upset about something that is happening in your personal or work life, ask yourself the following questions. After you complete the thoughts component of the exercise, it will be time to move on to the behavioral component.

Thoughts Identification and Response Exercise

Part One: Thoughts Component

1. What situation or event may have led to your feeling like this?

_____

_____

2. What are you telling yourself about the situation?

_____

_____

3. How accurate are those thoughts?

_____

_____

4. What evidence do you have that supports those thoughts?

_____

_____

5. What evidence do you have that disputes those thoughts?

_____

_____

6. What is a more accurate view of the situation?

_____

_____

Part Two: Behavioral Component

1. Define a plan to deal with the identified problems or issues.

_____

_____

2. Break the plan down into discrete steps (and define the steps).

_____

_____

3. Identify the thoughts that interfere with successfully completing each step you've set down. If you find that you are having difficulty identifying the thoughts that might get in the way, try using a visual image. This involves closing your eyes and visualizing yourself enacting your plan. By doing this, you will be able to imagine yourself in the situation, and it will help you identify the thoughts that might come up as you try to implement your plan.

4 Once you have identified these negative thoughts, use the Thoughts Identification and Response Exercise to move beyond them. Respond to your thoughts in a way that allows you to move forward. Use this process as you go through each step of your plan to ensure that negative thinking will not prevent you from successfully implementing the plan you have devised to deal with the problem.

5. As you complete each step of your plan, acknowledge your success. Giving yourself credit for what you are doing will encourage you to continue along the path to your goal.

• • •

Using the Thoughts Identification and Response Exercise: An Example

Rachel, a Caregiver, is a thirty-year-old sales manager for an insurance company. She used the Thoughts Identification and Response Exercise to understand her behavior regarding a situation at work. Rachel realized that she was irritable and edgy with her family as well as with her coworkers. She was having a hard time falling asleep at night and was waking up earlier than usual. As she became aware of these symptoms, she tried to recall when they had begun and what might have triggered them. Using the Thoughts Identification and Response Exercise, she identified her problem and developed a plan of action to deal with it.

1. *What situation or event may have led to me feeling like this?*
   Rachel realized that her symptoms began shortly after she was informed that her company had merged with another company and that she was going to be the manager of the combined sales departments. She was worried about the larger staff and additional responsibilities she would be expected to handle.

2. *What are you telling yourself about the situation?*
   Rachel was able to recognize that she was telling herself that she would not be able to handle the increased responsibilities. She also believed that she would be terrible at managing so many people and that they would all hate her.

3. *How accurate are those thoughts?*
   Rachel believed that her thinking about the upcoming situation was accurate, but she decided to look at the evidence for and against her thoughts.

4. *What evidence do you have that supports those thoughts?*
   She was unable to come up with any evidence to support her negative thoughts about the situation. Looking back over her career, she could not remember a single time when she was unable to meet her responsibilities, even when the demands upon her increased. As for her management style, no one working under her supervision had ever hated her.

5. *What evidence do you have that disputes those thoughts?*
   Rachel realized that throughout her career, she had sought out new and more demanding challenges and had lived up to and exceeded her bosses' expectations. She has a management style that enables her to get along with

her coworkers. She saw that, if anything, she bends over too much to make sure people are happy with their jobs and enjoy working with her.

6. *What is a more accurate view of the situation?*
    Rachel now realizes that she will be able to handle this new job and deal with the demands of a larger workforce. She is nervous about the change because it involves more responsibility than she has handled before, but she knows she has the skills to do it.

She then moved on to the behavioral component of the exercise. She began working on a plan to meet her new job demands. She broke the plan down into stages and tried to anticipate any thoughts or problems that might interfere with her execution of that plan. When she did identify a negative thought, she used the Thoughts Identification and Response Exercise to analyze and change it so that it would not decrease her ability to implement her plan. As Rachel took each step on the path to her goal, she gave herself positive reinforcement by acknowledging her accomplishments up to that point. Once Rachel was able to identify and control her ideas about how she would handle the new job situation, her mood improved and her sleep patterns returned to normal. Using the Thoughts Identification and Response Exercise will enable you to take more control of your life and to deal with the situations you encounter every day.

The Relationship Between Self-Concept and Self-Esteem

The previous exercise addressed problems that arise on a daily basis, at work and in your personal life. The following redefining exercise will be useful in changing your underlying beliefs instead of just your beliefs about a specific situation. A change in these deeply held or core beliefs will give you a better understanding of your skills and your strengths.

We have all heard the terms *self-concept* and *self-esteem*. Many times, these terms are used interchangeably. It is not uncommon for women to come to us hoping to improve their self-esteem. In order to accomplish this task, we have found that we must first help them to understand the difference between self-concept and self-esteem. In short, *self-concept* can be defined as an individual's picture of herself, and *self-esteem* refers to the value we place on that picture. We communicate both of these concepts to others by what we say about ourselves and our abilities and by what we do. If we do not have a good opinion of ourselves, we transmit that message in our interactions and it becomes the basis for the way others treat us.

Imagine wearing a sign across your chest that says "Ignore me, disregard me, discount what I say. I don't value me, so why should you?" It is important to understand that before we can feel that we are valued by others, we must first value ourselves.

The Redefining Process: An Example

Before we can begin the work of increasing our clients' self-esteem, we must help them to clearly define and examine their self-concept, or the picture they have of themselves. We have identified this as a Redefining Process. The first step in this process is listing the many characteristics that make up each person's picture of herself. In some ways, this is analogous to painting a self-portrait. We will now take you through this process with Kate, a Survivor.

Kate stated that she felt insecure and wanted to improve her self-esteem. When asked to describe herself, she listed the following characteristics: shy, not smart, easily intimidated, inadequate, and boring. She could not think of any strengths or positive characteristics. As she became aware of the picture she had of herself, she began to understand why her self-esteem was so low. She realized that it would be difficult, if not impossible, to value herself if she focused only on her negative aspects. Once Kate became aware of this negative picture, she was ready to begin the process of changing that picture, or her self-concept, and improving her self-esteem. This involved the following steps.

1. Identifying her beliefs about herself

2. Identifying the origins of those beliefs

3. Evaluating the accuracy of those beliefs

4. Identifying her strengths or positive characteristics

5. Painting a more realistic, balanced picture of herself

Kate's completed redefining exercise follows:

Step 1: Identifying her beliefs about herself

Kate believed that she was shy, not smart, inadequate, and boring. She also described herself as easily intimidated by others, especially those she perceived as being in positions of authority.

Step 2: Identifying the origins of those beliefs

Kate was able to remember that as a child, she saw herself as reticent, quiet, and shy. She remembers feeling insecure because of her learning disability. As she grew into adolescence, she became more and more hesitant about speaking up because she believed that anything she had to say was unimportant and incorrect. She began to think of herself as dumb and states that she did not have a very high opinion of herself. She was intimidated by teachers and afraid to speak up in class for fear of being wrong or embarrassing herself. As Kate described her childhood and adolescence, we saw the price she had paid and was continuing to pay for her problems at school.

Kate began to understand that her current beliefs about herself were the combined results of the messages she had received from her family and her teachers. In our work together, Kate was able to see that these messages were the foundation of the insecurity and hesitancy she exhibited in most areas of her life.

Step 3: Evaluating the accuracy of those beliefs

In order to do this, Kate first listed her beliefs, then subjected them to evaluation by examining the evidence that either supported or disputed those beliefs.

Belief #1: I'm shy.
Supporting Evidence: When I'm with other people, I'm uncomfortable, I don't know what to say, and I hesitate to speak up.
Disputing Evidence: I'm not like that with everyone. When I'm with people I know, I'm much more comfortable and have no problem participating in conversations. The only time I'm quiet is when I'm with people I perceive as authority figures, and that is due to all the old tapes I have about not speaking up. But I'm going to be working on this because now I know that I have the right to express myself.

Belief #2: I'm not smart.
Supporting Evidence: I didn't do well in high school. I didn't go to college. My parents said I would never amount to anything.
Disputing Evidence: I didn't do well in high school because I was too intimidated by the teachers to speak up and ask questions when I needed help. It was my fear of authority figures and of being wrong that kept me stuck. I didn't go to college because of my insecurity, which was a result of my

learning problem. I feel as though I had no guidance either at home or at school. I realize now that my lack of education was not due to a lack of intelligence on my part; instead, it was due to my fears and the lack of support I had as a teenager. Despite everything, I have been very successful in my job. I handle my workload well and have continually received excellent reviews from my supervisors. In addition to positive evaluations and pay raises, I have also been given the opportunity to advance.

Belief #3: I'm inadequate.

Supporting Evidence: My coworker works full-time and attends graduate school in the evenings. I can hardly handle working, let alone think of carrying a full load of college courses. I'm feeling totally stressed just from working. I would like to change jobs but have not done anything to begin the process. I know that other people are smarter than I am and have better work experience than I have. I'm probably not as good as the other people who would be applying for the same kind of job. I don't seem to be able to handle things as well as other people.

Disputing Evidence: The stress I'm experiencing is due to a very difficult work environment where I'm monitored constantly and treated like a robot. Despite the fact that I'm unhappy in my present position, I know I'm doing a good job, and I have received good evaluations from my supervisors. It's not true that I can't handle things; in addition to the work stress, I'm also taking care of my apartment and taking one course every semester in an effort to get my associate's degree. Although I'd like to find a new job, I've decided not to actively look for one since the company is paying for my courses. Therefore, I've decided to hang in here until I earn my associate's degree. I have to remember that I'm doing many things, and I'm doing them well.

Belief #4: I'm boring.

Supporting Evidence: When I'm at work, very few people come over and talk with me, but they all seem to enjoy talking among themselves. I hardly have any conversations with my boss, yet he's very friendly to my coworkers. Most people don't talk to me at parties. They all seem more interested in having conversations with other people. When people do talk to me, they seem eager to move on to somebody else. I never seem to know what to talk about and I'm quiet much of the time, so there are a lot of lulls in the conversation.

Disputing Evidence: When I'm at work, I'm so stressed and worried about doing a good job that I shut myself off from everyone. People aren't talking to me because I'm not encouraging them to, not because I'm boring. As far as my boss is concerned, it goes back to my old problem of not speaking up to anyone in authority for fear of looking stupid. I freeze up whenever he talks with me, and that does not make for much good conversation. I can see that my lack of socializing at work has more to do with my fears about authority figures and my tendency to isolate myself instead of the fact that I'm boring. When I'm with people I know, I'm comfortable and have no trouble talking to them and holding their interest.

Following the above examination of Kate's beliefs about herself, she had a clearer understanding of where her beliefs originated. The process helped her differentiate between the problems that were really hers and the ones that were a function of the society, culture, and family in which she lived. We refer to this process as "putting the pathology where it belongs." For instance, when her mother and father continually corrected what she said and did, Kate developed the belief that she was inadequate, that nothing she ever did was good enough. What Kate discovered was that her parents' condemnation was an expression of their concern about her; it was their way of trying to motivate her to improve and be more successful.

Step 4: Identifying her strengths or positive characteristics

As our work progressed, Kate was able to come up with the following list of her strengths.

- I am responsible.

- I care about other people.

- I work hard at everything I do.

- I am sensitive to other people's feelings.

- I usually complete whatever I start.

- I am a good friend.

Her ongoing assignment was to continue to add to this list and review the list at least twice daily as if she were taking a prescription: one reading in the morning and one reading at night.

Step 5: Painting a more realistic, balanced picture of herself

In order to do this, Kate had to incorporate all the information she had gathered in the first four steps. She took this information and created the following list, which was a verbal depiction of the new picture, or self-concept, she was developing. She had begun the process of redefining her way of thinking about herself. Kate divided her list into three categories.

Things I Like about Myself

- I am a responsible person.

- I am a good worker.

- I am a good employee.

- I see things through to completion.

- I care about other people.

- I am sensitive to other people's needs.

- I am a good friend.

- I am a good daughter and sister.

Things I Will Work to Change

- I will practice being more assertive by expressing my thoughts and needs.

- I will continue to remind myself that I am not a child and no longer need to be afraid of authority figures.

- I will try to initiate conversations with my boss when it is appropriate.

- I will try not to isolate myself at work and to participate in conversation with my coworkers.

Things I Have Come to Accept About Myself

- I am a quiet person.

- I prefer being with a few people I know and like rather than with large groups of people.

- At work, I tend to be a perfectionist, but I believe that helps me succeed.

Once Kate identified the negative beliefs she holds about herself, she then evaluated the accuracy of those beliefs. Using Cognitive Therapy tools, Kate looked at the evidence in her experiences that either supported or disputed these beliefs. With this process, she was able to accurately identify the characteristics she considered negative and wanted to change. This gave her the opportunity to take action. She developed a plan of attack, using both cognitive and behavioral exercises. She also identified those characteristics that she chose to accept.

Kate then combined her list of reevaluated negative characteristics from step 3 with the list of positive characteristics she had developed with step 4 to create a more complete picture of herself. This picture encompassed a variety of aspects and provided a balanced perspective. She was able to recognize her good qualities as well as those that were not as good. Most important, Kate no longer defined herself totally in terms of her negative characteristics. She saw her flaws as part of being human, not inadequate. This revised picture led to an improved sense of self-worth, which affected her style of interacting with other people and the quality of their responses to her.

Redefining Yourself

While it is interesting to read about a process and see how it works for someone else, we have found that it is much more valuable for each individual to engage in the process herself. The following exercise will help you become aware of your self-concept and enable you to change that picture if you so desire. We suggest that you write down your responses to these exercises on a separate sheet of paper, so you will be able to clearly delineate all the information you need as you redefine your picture of yourself.

Redefining Exercise

1. **List your beliefs about yourself.**

    _____

    _____

2. **Where did these beliefs come from? What messages did you get from your family, friends, and teachers?**

    _____

    _____

3. **How accurate are these beliefs? (List each belief, followed by the supporting evidence and the disputing evidence.)**

_____

_____

4 **What are your strengths or positive characteristics?**

_____

_____

5. **Describe yourself more accurately.**

   What do you like about yourself? _____

   What are the things you will try to change? _____

   What are the things you have come to accept about yourself?

   _____

● ● ●

Completing the Redefining Exercise will have a positive impact on how you function at work and in all areas of your life.

Women and the Imposter Syndrome

For some women, negative thinking gives rise to self-doubts, which interfere with their ability to wholeheartedly acknowledge their accomplishments. Self-doubts also provide the basis for a condition known as the Imposter Syndrome.

If a woman has negative beliefs about herself, she frequently finds it difficult to acknowledge her abilities. Her conviction that she is somehow deficient in comparison to others can be heard in statements such as "Other people seem to have more going for them than I do." She places a very high value on the skills and abilities she sees in others, meanwhile denying the possibility that she herself may be as exceptional as the people she admires.

A woman who suffers from the Imposter Syndrome experiences intense self-doubt and tends to minimize her intellectual ability. On the occasions when she does risk speaking out on an issue, she worries constantly about whether or not she looked foolish while she was speaking her mind (Stiver, 1991). Was she too aggressive? Should she have refrained from making a comment at all? She places her behavior under a microscope, and this intense scrutiny often prevents her from expressing her thoughts. When she is recognized by others for making a valuable comment, she begins to wonder how she managed to fool them. She attributes her successes to luck but will take full responsibility for her failures.

Some women are intimately aware of this dance going on in their heads and are annoyed with themselves for doing it. Yet they steadfastly retain their beliefs that they are fooling others and that they do not know as much as others think they know. Despite much evidence to the contrary, they hold on to the fear that at some point the game will be over and they will be recognized as frauds.

"When people tell me I've accomplished so much, I just sort of shrug my shoulders. I do believe that I have accomplished some things, but I don't believe it's as special as people tell me. I had dinner last night with a person who has been my client for many years. He was wrestling with a difficult business problem and said to me, 'Nobody understands this the way you understand it. Do you have any concept of how special you are in your capability?' You don't recognize the fact that what you do is special. You think everybody does this, can do this, if they only try hard enough. They can't. They don't." Jane—a Maverick

Women who experience the Imposter Syndrome undervalue themselves. This is evident in the experience of one of our interviewees, Jane, a Maverick.

In order to break free of such strong self-doubts, women must become aware of their strengths and integrate them into their daily lives. Slowly, confidence will grow, and an improved sense of self will emerge. Integration is the key. We must integrate positive aspects of ourselves into our personal and professional lives. We work hard as women, in all of our roles—as friends, mothers, sisters, significant others, workers, leaders, and colleagues—to acquire and accumulate knowledge. We implement what we have learned and successfully carry out these different roles. Yet, we have a tendency to minimize and devalue our abilities. By doing so, we aren't giving ourselves a chance. We convince ourselves that we do not deserve a certain position, promotion, or relationship because we have been conditioned to believe that we might not measure up, that others are better than we are and therefore we are not to be valued. This becomes a self-fulfilling prophecy, which leads us into a downward spiral of negativity, hopelessness, and, at times, depression.

It is important to recognize that it is the perspective we take of a situation that is negative, not our ability or behavior. If we do not believe that we are of value, that we have abilities and competencies, why should anyone else? In order for others to value and respect us, we must first value and respect oruselves. When we think more positively about ourselves, we tend to present in a more confident manner, and in turn, others treat us with more respect. If you think the Imposter Syndrome describes you, the following exercise should help you recognize the difference between your negative perspective and your positive abilities and behavior.

The Imposter Syndrome Exercise

1. **Do you sometimes think of yourself as an imposter at work?**

_____

_____

2. **In what ways do you feel like an imposter?**

_____

_____

3. **What thoughts about yourself lead you to believe that you are an imposter?**

_____

_____

4. **What evidence do you have from your work experience that supports this view of yourself?**

_____

_____

5. **What evidence do you have from your work experience that disputes this view of yourself?**

_____

_____

● ● ●

We hope that the information in this chapter has helped you become more aware of the ways in which your thinking affects your functioning at work. It is vital that you have an understanding of how your environments, past and present, have influenced your ideas about yourself. Knowledge of yourself and your environment offers you the power and opportunity to change your self-concept. Utilizing Cognitive Therapy processes such as the Thoughts Identification and Response Exercise and the Redefining Exercise will enable you to take control of your life. In the next chapter, we will discuss and provide tools that will assist you in making behavioral changes in all areas of your life.

11   CHANGING THE WAY WE ACT

Before you can begin to implement change in your life, you must first take stock of what you are currently doing and whether or not it is working for you. In the previous chapter, we walked you through a process for changing your thinking. Now that you have a better understanding of the thoughts that motivate your behaviors, we will focus on behavioral change. The following exercise will help you recognize and determine which behaviors you need to stop, which behaviors you need to start, and which behaviors you need to continue. This exercise serves as a starting point and will give you a good sense of where to go from here.

Behavior Evaluation Exercise

	In Your Personal Life	In Your Professional Life
What are the behaviors you need to stop?	_____ _____	_____ _____
What are the behaviors you need to start?	_____ _____	_____ _____
What are the behaviors you need to continue?	_____ _____	_____ _____

●   ●   ●

Once you have identified the behaviors you need to stop, start, and continue, you must create a plan for behavioral change. The steps of the plan should be specific and detailed, and you must adhere strictly to the timeline. Consider the following process when you are designing your personal plan.

Behavioral Change Plan

1. Identify the behavior you wish to change.

2. Delineate the steps required to make this change.

3. Create a timeline for implementing these steps.

4. Determine the obstacles that might interfere with your taking these steps and making the change.

5. Formulate a plan of action to address these obstacles.

6. Establish a support system to help you through this process of change.

7. Practice the new behavior on a regular basis.

Without a behavioral change plan, it is easy to feel overwhelmed and uncertain about how to implement change in your life. The Behavioral Change Plan will be your guide to thinking through the necessary steps. In addition to developing a plan for changing your behavior, there are several other behavioral strategies you may find helpful as you work on altering the way you function.

Behavioral Change Strategies

The following are some strategies for implementing behavioral change in your life.

Behavioral Experiments

Once you have decided on a new behavior, set up an opportunity to experiment with it and collect data about the results. People often anticipate a negative outcome to any new behavior they are considering and decide not to try it. We encourage you to write down what you're expecting before you actually engage in the new behavior, then write down what really happened when you did. Most people are pleasantly surprised that, most of the time, trying out a new positive behavior resulted in a positive consequence.

For example, Lisa, a Peacekeeper, was upset because her boss continually ridiculed her in front of her coworkers. When we suggested that she speak with him privately about how she felt and how she wanted to be treated, she replied that she was uncomfortable about doing so because she feared he would treat her even worse if she spoke up. After much discussion and planning, she agreed to try this experiment. She set up an appointment to speak with her boss, then wrote down her anticipated negative consequences. Her meeting with the boss went well, and he apologized for his behavior. Afterward, he treated her in a respectful manner when he spoke to her and no longer demeaned her in front of her coworkers. Because she had the courage to conduct this behavioral exercise, Lisa accomplished two things. First, she learned that her negative anticipation of events was inaccurate, and second, she went on to develop a mutually respectful relationship with her boss.

Problem Solving

Many people spend countless hours worrying about a problem or a situation. This accomplishes nothing and instead often leads to anxiety and depression. Action, as opposed to worrying, is the key to solving problems. In order to take action, you must move from a worrying mode to a problem-solving mode. The cognitive method of identifying what you are telling yourself about the issue and then developing a different perspective by examining the evidence will assist you in switching modes. Once you have switched modes, the following steps will help you deal effectively with the problem. It is often helpful to do this with a friend, family member, or coworker.

1. Identify the problem: This process requires that you identify the exact issues you are concerned about and the specific factors that are maintaining the problem. Think in concrete and specific terms because that kind of thinking will help you move on to ways of solving the problem.

2. Brainstorm: Generate and record as many possible solutions to the problem as you can, regardless of their feasibility.

3. Evaluate: Now go back over your list of possible solutions and evaluate them one by one. Consider the positives and negatives for each, then list them on a chart to help you in the evaluation process. Once you have identified one or two good solutions, you are ready to move on to implementing one of them.

4. Implementation: Break the plan down into specific steps. Identify any problems that may interfere with carrying out those specific steps and be prepared to deal with them.

5. Congratulate yourself: After you have dealt with the problem to the best of your ability, acknowledge your efforts, regardless of the outcome. Give yourself a pat on the back for becoming a problem solver instead of a worrier! Doing something about a problem instead of worrying about it frees up a lot of time that you can spend on activities you enjoy.

Communication Style

Many women are hesitant to state what is on their minds in a clear and concise fashion because they believe that doing so would lead to conflict. There is nothing confrontational about stating your needs and thoughts. We all have the right to do that. It is important to recognize that speaking up for yourself does not have to appear confrontational. Recognizing the difference between assertiveness and aggressiveness will help you develop a method of stating your thoughts and standing up for yourself in a nonconfrontational manner. Aggressive communication lashes out at other people in a manner that shows disrespect and sets the stage for confrontation. It often results when the anger and frustration that build up from not speaking out and feeling belittled finally cause an explosion. Assertive communication expresses your thoughts in a direct, straightforward manner while at the same time respecting the rights of others.

Another earmark of assertive expression is making statements without qualifying them in some fashion. For example, how often have you heard yourself or someone you know say some of the following? "I could be wrong, but I do not think that will work." "I'm not good with numbers, but I think you made a mistake on this check." "I could be mistaken, but I believe our appointment was for today." Qualifying your statements diminishes the power of what you have said and consequently your own power and effectiveness. Stating these same thoughts without the qualifiers displays a self-confidence that demands respect from the listener. "I do not think that will work." "I think you made a mistake on this check." "I believe our appointment was for today." People will listen and respond to your statements with respect if you communicate conviction rather than apology.

Strengths List

In order to develop self-validation, you must first recognize your strengths. An effective list should include the strengths that enable you to function successfully in all areas of your life. Most women tend to take their strengths for granted and focus on what they believe to be their weaknesses. Using this strengths list will help you reprogram your way of thinking about yourself. We suggest that this list be readily available so that you can read it at least twice a day. Many women find that the night table is a good place to keep it because they will remember to read it in the morning when they get up and in the evening when they go to bed. If you put it in a drawer or bury it in your pocketbook, you will probably forget to read it. Think of this as a prescription with no negative side effects.

Being Good to Yourself

In order to do your best at work, you must keep your mind sharp and your body sound. We think this is one of the most important suggestions we can offer. Too many of us put ourselves last on our list of people we have to care for and things we have to do. When we suggest that they take better care of themselves, many women respond by saying that they do not have the time. Make the time—you are worth it, you need it, and you deserve it!

We often tell our clients to think of themselves as cars. A car gets us where we have to go and helps us deal with the demands and responsibilities of daily living. But what happens when you do not take care of that car by putting in gas and oil? The car stops and can no longer be of use to anyone. We as women are similar to cars in that we provide vital services for most of the people in our lives. There is nothing selfish about spending time to take care of ourselves. When we do not take care of ourselves, we eventually become run-down and burned out. At that point, we are not of much help to anyone, especially ourselves.

The first step in this process is to identify what you need and what would nourish and replenish you each day. Make a list of things you would like to do for yourself but have been putting off for one reason or another. Here are some suggestions to get you started.

1. Work some downtime into your day, some time that is just for you, with no demands or responsibilities. It does not have to be a lot of time; it just has to be yours. During your downtime, you could soak in a bubble bath, curl up in a comfortable spot and read a book, watch a favorite television program, listen to music, or just daydream.

2. Exercise—it's good for the body and the mind. Exercise works off anxiety and tension while it tones the body, helping you to stay healthy. Whether you prefer to work out at home or at the gym, the benefits far outweigh the costs. Walking is another great way to exercise. All it requires is a decent pair of walking shoes and your ability to give yourself permission to do something for yourself. Take a walk, get outside and breathe in the fresh air, feel how good it can be.

3. Relax your mind and body with deep, slow breathing and visual imagery. We like to suggest combining these processes into one relaxing experience. Once you have mastered them, you can use them at any time and in any way to help you relax when you are tense. Find a quiet, comfortable spot where you can either sit or lie down, then clear your mind. Once you are feeling at ease and your mind is clear, begin taking long, slow, deep breaths: inhale to the count of 4, hold the breath for a count of 4, then exhale to the count of 4. Repeat this breathing exercise 10 times and notice the relaxed feeling that begins to move through your body. Continue with the breathing and

begin thinking of a peaceful place where you have been or would like to go, then close your eyes and visualize yourself there. Some people use a beach scene; others, a park; while others see themselves relaxing in their backyards. Once you have picked your scene, utilize your senses to immerse yourself in the setting. Listen to the sounds you hear there, smell the smells, and look at the scenery until you feel more and more connected to this peaceful place. Continue your slow breathing and visualizing and enjoy your mental vacation. When you open your eyes, you will feel refreshed, and any tension you were experiencing before will be gone.

We hope that you will take the time to try some of the cognitive and behavioral strategies we have presented. We know that if you work at these suggestions on a regular basis, you will be on the path to implementing change in your life. There are other areas in which you can implement change at work. In the remainder of this chapter, we will discuss suggestions regarding self-promotion, development as a leader, mentoring, and evaluating the fit between yourself and your company.

Women and Self-Promotion

Self-promotion refers to one's ability to move forward by clearly stating one's skills, strengths, wants, and needs in a direct, matter-of-fact way. Based on our conversations with women, we have identified a few factors that may interfere with a woman's ability to promote herself. Many women are uncomfortable with self-promotion because it flies in the face of society's message that a woman is the support person who is supposed to put other people's needs ahead of her own. Women must begin to realize that caring about themselves is not selfish, nor does it make them unavailable to care for others. Think of how you support your best friend, then do that for yourself. One purpose of this book is to help you become your own best friend.

Many women think that promoting themselves is a form of competition. This presents a conflict because most women are not comfortable with competition; they view it as divisive and isolating, two qualities that run counter to their need to be connected and in relationship with the people in their lives. Women must alter their perspective on self-promotion and competition in order to advance themselves professionally. Self-promotion is not about competition; it's about making the most of your own potential.

"I want a seat at the management table and I don't know whether that will happen or not. I decided to articulate that goal aggressively because there's a lot of jockeying going on now. There's a new guy joining the company, and he has been very explicit about wanting a leadership position. I've seen a lot of deference being paid to how he feels. They're not paying attention to how I feel because they don't know how I feel. If I want something, I need to promote myself in order to get it. I can't sit back and hope it will happen. I have to actively express what I want." **Jane—a Maverick**

In our work, we have seen many intelligent, competent women who are unaware of their strengths and capabilities. Their comments reflect self-doubt, which emanates from an underlying sense of inadequacy. This sense of inadequacy is a stumbling block to self-promotion. Women need to acknowledge the strengths they bring to the workplace. Strengths are often taken for granted, seen as par for the course, not as something special that should be considered of value to yourself and others. This inability to appreciate their own positive qualities contributes to the formation and preservation of women's unclear sense of self and accomplishment.

Another factor that may discourage a woman from engaging in self-promotion is lack of awareness about what it takes to advance. Many women believe that doing their jobs to the best of their ability will lead to advancement in the company. Often, however, it does not. Women must become more aware of the importance of articulating the kind of work they are doing, their skills, and their vision in regard to progressing in the organization.

Some women represent the other end of the continuum. These women are comfortable with self-promotion and subsequently achieve success in their respective fields. These women have identified their own needs and given voice to them. In the past, this type of behavior was synonymous with selfishness. In reality, these women are defining a goal and a vision for themselves and acting on it. Think about a time at work when you were in a meeting with a group of colleagues and upper management, and one of your colleagues engaged in active self-promotion. What was the outcome? How did senior management respond to this person? How did it make you feel? We often jump to conclusions about how to behave based on our own ideas about what is comfortable for us. The way we think about ourselves affects our behavior as well as our beliefs about the behavior of others. It is important to sit back and collect data through observation in order to determine the accuracy of our beliefs. The following Self-Promotion Exercise will help you examine your thoughts about your behavior and the behavior of others.

Self-Promotion Exercise

1. **Do you promote yourself at work? If yes, how? If not, why not?**

   _____

   _____

2. **What are the beliefs that keep you from self-promotion?**

   _____

   _____

3. **What is the evidence that supports those beliefs?**

   _____

   _____

4. **What will be the consequence of self-promotion for you?**

   _____

   _____

5. **What are the consequences you have observed when others engage in self-promotion?**

   _____

   _____

· · ·

Self-confidence is a significant factor in successful and comfortable self-promotion. In order to promote yourself, you need to be aware of the skills and strengths you possess. Not only do you need to be aware of your assets, you also need to be able to articulate them to others. While it is wonderful to know that you possess all kinds of skills and strengths, these qualities will remain your secret if you never tell anyone about them. The powerful combination of self-confidence and self-promotion are two important keys to developing yourself as a leader.

Strategies for Developing Your Leadership Style

Regardless of your position at work, you are always interacting with coworkers. Whether you are taking direction or giving direction, you are continually engaging in leadership behaviors. The following suggestions for developing a leadership style may be helpful to you. Whether you are an up-and-coming leader or have acted in this role for some time, consider integrating the following strategies into your own leadership style.

- Develop and communicate a vision and strategy for your colleagues, work group, or project team. As a leader, you must be sure that your vision is consistent with that of the organization. This type of thinking will set you apart, and others will come to see you in a leadership role.

- Set goals for yourself (and for your work group or department, if applicable). When you establish a plan for achieving your goals, others will see you as a focused person who gets things done.

- Think like a leader. View problems as opportunities and think in terms of solutions. Thinking like a leader means you must trust your instincts, think strategically about the business and your customers, and bring creativity to solving problems and making decisions.

- Communicate effectively. A leader must be clear and concise in her messages and directives. The keys to successful leadership communication are self-confidence, eye contact, and an approachable style. A leader must also be a good listener. It is important to understand the thoughts, concerns, and suggestions of coworkers. Remember that listening is at least as important as speaking, for a great leader knows what she does not know and is open to learning all that she can from others.

- Develop future leaders. The mark of a truly great leader is her ability to develop future leaders. She is concerned about her own success as well as the success of others and the company. In order to develop future leaders, you must be keenly aware of your own strengths and skills and help your protégé acknowledge and utilize her own. Developing future leaders—by sharing the story of how you attained your position, as well as the factors that influence and enhance your style—will further sharpen your own leadership abilities. Leaders who are interested in the professional development of others are particularly effective mentors.

Women and Mentoring

Mentoring is a relationship between two people that focuses on the personal and professional growth of the protégé. A mentor can be several levels above or at the same level as her protégé if she has a wealth of experience. The mentor advises the protégé on how to navigate the waters of organizational culture and politics. She helps the protégé identify career goals and assists her in getting from the spot she currently occupies in her career to the position or situation she hopes to attain.

A mentoring relationship can be formal or informal. More and more organizations are instituting formal mentoring programs in order to reduce turnover, heighten a sense of connection between the employee and the organization, develop future leaders, and retain female employees. The purpose of an informal mentoring relationship is similar; however, an informal mentoring relationship develops when individuals with mutual interests make their own decision to work together. An informal mentor may or may not work for the same company as the protégé.

Men are more likely than women to have mentors (Wood, 1994), and women without mentors are at a disadvantage in terms of their job effectiveness and prospects for career advancement (Noe, 1988). Since there are fewer women at senior levels, fewer female mentors are available. That is not to say that a woman cannot have a male mentor. A woman looking for a mentor can team up with a male mentor, but a mentor should function, in part, as a role model. It may be difficult for a male mentor to be a role model for a woman. Female mentors may be better at assisting women protégés with issues such as handling a masculine culture and balancing work and personal life.

When they think of mentoring, women see the relationship as one that is intertwined with friendship and connection, whereas men generally view mentoring as

"The mentoring program within my department is different from that of the larger organization. It's informal. We have a buddy system that is separate from the larger organization's formal coaching process. In the buddy system, people just connect with the people they connect with. It's kind of a network as far as who goes to whom to deal with project or personal concerns. My two senior managers are very accessible to the junior people, and they work hard to be that way. It's a migrating process. There's a lot of support for career planning and helping with the work. I spend a lot of time with the junior people in my department, a lot of hands-on time, not a formal coaching process. I work with them on projects and talk with them about their lives. I like to be involved in the work. I'm there in the trenches and that allows mentoring to take place in a different way." **Jane—a Maverick** a task-oriented alliance (Burke and McKeen, 1990). Women's view of the mentoring relationship is consistent with their style of interaction. They tend to see relationships as an opportunity to connect with others.

The women with whom we spoke stated that formal mentoring programs are on the rise within their respective organizations. Many reported a formal program as well as an informal process whereby individuals in their respective departments or business units gravitate toward potential mentors. Gone are the days when mentors quietly observed potential protégés before making their selections. Protégés are now actively involved in the mentor selection process.

When asked about her own experience in being mentored, Jane offered the following comment. "I would love to have a woman mentor me, and to be able to look up to her. When I began working there were few female mentors available. I would have liked to have had one."

Many people have found mentoring to be beneficial in their professional lives. The following questions may be helpful to you as you seek out a mentoring relationship.

Mentoring Exercise

1. **Do you have a mentor?**

   _____

   _____

2. **How would a mentor be helpful to you?**

   _____

   _____

3. **What would you look for in a good mentor?**

   _____

   _____

4. **Are you a mentor for others?**

   _____

   _____

5. What makes you a good mentor?

_____

_____

• • •

Mentoring is a way of educating employees about the culture and structure of the organization. In addition, a mentor can be a valuable resource in evaluating the fit between yourself and your employer.

Evaluating the Fit

As we discussed earlier in this book, each societal group has a set of rules or "should's" that delineate the kind of behavior that's expected if people wish to fit into that particular group. Companies are no exception. If you hope to succeed as a member of an organization, you must be aware of its rules or "should's." The organizational "should's" detail a pattern of behavior that the company expects its employees to follow. Once you are aware of the organizational rules or "should's" and have determined whether or not you fit in, you have the option of making one of the following choices.

1. If you do not fit into the organization, what are you willing to do to accommodate the organization's demands?

2. Can you find a way of fitting in without having to hide who you really are?

3. Should you seek employment elsewhere?

In deciding the correctness of the fit between yourself and the organization, you must first be aware of your needs. Completing a self-inventory is a good way to do this. We suggest that you take the time to write these things down in order to give this process the attention it deserves. Once you finish your self-inventory, you can complete the same type of chart for your company or the company you are considering joining. This chart would have the following columns: the positives about your job, the interests of your coworkers, the company's prevailing communication style, and its environment. When you evaluate the company's environment, think in terms of how much freedom and support are available to help you attain your goals. After you complete both of these charts, you can compare them; you will then be in a better position to determine whether or not this company meets your needs

PEG'S SELF-INVENTORY

Strengths	Interests	Communication Style	Environment Needed	Goals
• Organized	• Helping others	• Direct	• Supportive	• Management position
• Dependable	• Community activities	• Respectful	• Individuals respected	• Recognition as a leader among colleagues
• Intelligent		• Considerate	• Employees valued	
• Self-directed	• Relationships with coworkers	• Good listener		
• Quick to learn			• Employee input encouraged	• Recognition as knowledgeable or expert in particular field

PEG'S COMPANY INVENTORY

Positives	Interests of Coworkers	Communication Style	Environment
• Pays well	• Self-promotion	• Direct	• Nonsupportive
• Good benefits	• Competition	• Authoritarian	• Competitive
• Friendships with coworkers	• Gossip	• Abrupt	• Employees devalued
• Convenient location		• Insensitive	
• Opportunity for advancement			

and consequently what your next step should be. Peg, a Survivor, utilized this process. Her charts are shown above.

After a careful review of both charts, Peg was able to see that her company's environment was not suited to her. This poor fit was the reason for her continual problems, but Peg had always believed that she was having difficulties because there was something wrong with her. She had personalized issues that were in reality discrepancies between her needs and her work environment. Because of this personalization, she developed negative beliefs about herself that contributed to her depressed mood and constant frustration at work. An objective appraisal of her work situation enabled her to remove the emotional component and deal with the issue at hand. She was able to ask herself the following question: "Does this environment provide me with what I need to be successful?" Once she examined the data in both charts, she was able to see that her present work environment did not meet her needs in terms of successfully achieving her goals. She then reviewed her options.

1. If I do not fit into the organization, what am I willing to do to accommodate the organization's demands?

2. Can I find a way of fitting in without having to hide who I really am?

3. Should I seek employment elsewhere?

After reviewing her options, Peg decided to seek employment elsewhere. Because she had completed a self-inventory, she was much more aware of her needs with regard to her professional life and utilized this information in her job search. This time, she was more discriminating about choosing the appropriate work environment for herself. She is currently employed with a company where she feels respected, valued, and appreciated. The environment is supportive and provides her with the opportunity for growth and advancement.

Like Peg, there are times when we all need to take stock of our lives, including our needs, strengths, abilities, and comfort level inside and outside of the workplace. When we do this, we afford ourselves greater control and are better able to apply our strengths. We are actively taking control of our lives rather than letting our lives take control of us. We often hear women say that they are victims of circumstance, stuck in situations in which they feel they have little or no control. While control may seem to elude us in those moments, it is there. It is just waiting—waiting for us to become aware of it and use it to change our lives for the better. It is crucial that we become more aware of our needs as individuals, what we enjoy, and what we are willing to live with and, sometimes, even to tolerate. Being comfortable with who we are and the environments in which we place ourselves is always the necessary first step to becoming more self-confident, successful, and happy. These are all gifts we can give ourselves. Some of us just need to give ourselves these gifts more often. Bringing a strong sense of yourself into social situations and the workplace will increase the likelihood that you will experience less stress within these environments.

In this chapter, we have presented behavioral strategies that will help you implement change in your life. They will help you to realize your goals and enhance your ability to succeed at work. We believe that the combination of the cognitive and behavioral chapters presents a powerful strategy and provides you with the tools you need to begin the process of change.

12   CREATING OUR FUTURE

As women seek to effect change in their lives, they must also take every opportunity to do the same in their workplaces. Oftentimes, individuals may feel that, as a single entity within the larger organization, they are too small to make a difference. This is far from true. Individuals may create change in a variety of ways at a grassroots level by identifying their needs and then voicing them to those in leadership positions. This process can be taken a step further by groups of women coming together to identify their collective needs and working to effect change.

Organizational Change

Both women and management must recognize the strengths women bring to the workplace. An organization that encourages women to function in accordance with their strengths will ultimately benefit from its policies. However, the ability to develop and maintain relationships is often ignored and devalued in the workplace by women themselves as well as by management. Women are expected to work and succeed according to the male values of separation and autonomy. This is equivalent to expecting a person to succeed without using her skills. Compromising the effectiveness of women in the workforce has a negative impact on the company's productivity and success and can lead to low morale, high turnover, and female flight from corporate America, thus depriving this country of a vast resource. The question becomes, how do companies stop this? How do companies make themselves more women-friendly?

They can begin by listening to the needs of their female employees and working to understand the changes that must occur in accordance with those needs. The increasing numbers of women in the workforce necessitate an altered perspective on the part of management. The old rules no longer apply. They inhibit the growth of companies as well as the professional growth of women. In order to change this perspective, those at the management and leadership levels would benefit from using the same cognitive strategies we have discussed throughout this book. Before behavioral change can begin, they must first examine their beliefs about employees in general and women in particular. Once they become aware of their beliefs, they can analyze them objectively to determine the effectiveness of their existing perspective and begin the process of behavioral change.

Change in any company will only be effective if leadership and upper management see the need for it, believe in it, and support it wholeheartedly. Viewing women's styles of working, managing, communicating, and leading as unique, not deficient, benefits everyone and can enhance a company's productivity and effectiveness. Many companies have already begun to see the need to create change in order to better utilize the resources that women bring to the workplace; however, much more remains to be done. Creating mentoring programs, instituting flexible working situations, and utilizing technology will result in environments that support balance between work and personal life. Additional options for initiating such change may include workshops to address differences in the work styles of men and women, as well as to examine the underlying management belief systems that may be preserving the status quo. More and more, companies are promoting women's participation in career development and planning programs and leadership development coaching.

Organizations need to think through the culture that permeates their hallways, staff meetings, and corporate communications such as the written and spoken messages crafted by leaders and received by the entire population of the company. These messages set the tone and provide directives for the organization and its members. Management needs to recognize the need to deliver messages that embrace the diversity of the workplace. Organizational demographics are constantly changing, with more women and minorities now represented. Given this shift in the workplace, the leaders of organizations need to maintain heightened sensitivity toward their employees.

Organizational leaders must be open to supporting change in the corporate culture. They will be able to do this if they recognize and understand why such change in thinking and attitude is necessary. Shifts in culture and thinking among leaders typically derive from a change in the needs of the organization's members or from the marketplace. Both serve as catalysts for organizational change. An example of a cultural shift in the workplace is the institution of flexible work arrangements due to the needs of working mothers. Flexible work arrangements as well as the use of new technologies, such as voice mail, e-mail, and videoconferencing, are responses to the needs of a changing workforce.

What Does All of This Mean for Our Daughters and Other Young Girls?

As women, our challenge for the future is to take what we learn in our respective lives and pass this knowledge on to our daughters or other young girls so that they may experience a different and perhaps better reality than the one we've known. We have so many options available to us today, thanks in large part to the women who went before us, who pioneered this myriad of opportunities. Now it's our turn to take on a similar role by educating today's young girls about all the choices we have at our disposal. We will be successful in this process as long as we first look inward and work to enhance our sense of self, thereby acting as role models to the next generation of young women.

As mother and daughter, we know from our own experience that the guidance and encouragement provided by parents and other role models exert a crucial influence on a young girl and her self-concept. Exposure to images of women as competent professionals, an environment that accepts the idea that a woman can achieve any goal if she works hard enough to attain it, and the opportunity to experiment with different hobbies, classes, and work situations can contribute to a young girl's conviction that her future is limitless. This combination of experiences helps her form a picture of who she is, what is important to her, and what she ultimately wants to be, both personally and professionally.

The roles we assume and the behaviors we model have a strong impact on girls growing up today. Are we raising young girls to believe they can be anything? Are we teaching them how to be successful in the roles they choose? Are we helping our daughters, nieces, sisters, and neighbors to realize at an early age what the choices are? Are we assisting them in carving out a path that is right for them? Girls learn to recognize and internalize their strengths through a combination of methods, which include storytelling, participating in a variety of activities, nurturing interests, and building self-esteem and confidence. In the process, they become whole and integrated individuals, personally and, eventually, professionally, with fully developed minds and interests of their own. In order to be a positive role model, you must believe in yourself and understand the roles you have assumed in your own life.

Recognizing Our Strengths

"My greatest strength is that people are important to me. You always need to have time in your life and in your work to listen to people. Hear what their concerns are, hear what they're upset about, and celebrate whatever wonderful events they experience. For the most part, I have been true to the notion that we are here for each other. That is my greatest strength, and I'm always conscious of it. I keep my office door open to let people know I'm here and available for them." **Rachel—a Caregiver**

"I'm very perceptive. I read people and situations very well, which gives me an advantage because I think I understand better."

Jane—a Maverick

Women exhibit strengths in their personal lives that enable them to perform the multiple tasks that make up their day. They prioritize, organize, empathize, listen, support, nurture, communicate, and empower. It is important to understand that we utilize these abilities in all aspects of our lives. Women are beginning to acknowledge that they bring these strengths to the workplace as well.

A woman must recognize the strengths she brings to bear in all that she does. By identifying her strengths, she develops an understanding of who she is and of the skills she has to offer, both personally and professionally. Acknowledging her strengths enhances self-confidence and self-esteem. It allows a woman to feel comfortable in her own skin, and she will then feel comfortable about making decisions. It sets the tone for how she will function as well as how she will be viewed and treated by others. She presents a picture of a complete person who is fully aware of her power and who likes the person she has become through her confident use of that power. Many women seem unable to articulate their strengths, or they may be unaware of the strengths they possess because they keep this part of themselves locked away. It is necessary for women to tear down the barriers that prevent them from acknowledging the value of their strengths, leaving them unable to implement those strengths in the workplace. Complete the following exercise to identify your strengths.

"I feel as though I have a good sense of myself. I feel very centered and confident about myself." **Lisa—a Peacekeeper**

"My strength is dealing with people. I'm no longer afraid to ask questions, or to do what I need to do to complete a project even when I'm unsure of how to go about it."

Kate—a Survivor

"Stamina. I think I have a creative/analytical mind that I can use in a number of ways—solving a technical problem, a personal problem, a sales problem, or a negotiation point."

Nancy—an Entrepreneur

Strength Awareness Exercise

1. **What strengths do you believe you have and use in your personal life?**

   _____

   _____

2. **What strengths do you bring to the workplace?**

   _____

   _____

3. **Are there similarities between the two lists?**

   _____

   _____

4. **Do you integrate the strengths you use in your personal life into your professional life? If yes, which ones? If no, what stops you from doing so?**

   _____

   _____

• • •

Your Role and the Future

Once upon a time, we were all little girls adapting to our respective environments—family, school, friends, and society. Today, as grown women, we must still adapt to our respective environments; however, we have more options available to us. We can create and choose the type of environment in which we live and work. Life is not a static situation but a series of dynamic, ever changing stages that requires each of us to adapt and evolve. It was this process of evolution that led to the development of our respective roles. As our lives progress from one stage to another, there may come a time when our roles should change as well. It is important to realize that the role behaviors that worked well for us at one time may not be the best ones now.

In order to determine if your role is working for you or if you should consider changing it, stop and think about how you feel at work. Do you find yourself getting angry or frustrated every day? Have you noticed a decreased desire to do your best? Do you think that your efforts are being acknowledged and valued by your boss, or do you feel that you are being taken advantage of and overlooked? Have you progressed as you had hoped toward your career goals? Your thoughts and feelings can be cues that the role you have assumed in the workplace may not be in your best interest and you may need to change your behaviors.

Of course, everyone reacts in her own way, but there are some specific cues experienced by people who fall into the various roles we have discussed. For example, the Peacekeeper, whose greatest strength is her ability to work with others and create consensus among her coworkers, may find herself feeling withdrawn and making herself unavailable to others. These behaviors are uncharacteristic of her role and indicate that something is not working for her. This awareness may be the first step in changing to a more balanced, effective style of behavior.

The following examples of cues may be helpful for the other roles. The Maverick, whose greatest strength is her belief in herself and her ability to work independently, may suffer at times from an overwhelming sense of isolation and lack of confidence. These feelings are cues to her that her typical behaviors are not working and she must take the time to explore possible changes to her style of work and interaction. The Pleaser, whose greatest strength is to be everything to everybody, may start to feel that people are taking advantage of her and become resentful. The Caregiver, whose primary focus is to be supportive of everyone, may begin to feel overwhelmed. The Survivor, whose strength has been her capacity to adapt to any situation, may start to experience feelings of victimization and anger. The Entrepreneur, whose greatest strength is her creativity and motivation, may feel stymied and unmotivated.

What are the cues that help you realize it is time to change your behavior? Which behaviors do you think you need to change? How do you think these changes will affect your success at work?

Throughout this book, we have stressed the need to understand the impact of your development on your growth as a woman and on the role you have assumed. We have discussed how familial and societal expectations affect the development of women. As a child, you may have been subject to many influences that led you to develop certain beliefs about yourself, which in turn resulted in the type of behavior you exhibited and the role you assumed in your family and at work. You were also exposed to many experiences and opportunities that helped you develop strengths, skills, and ideas about yourself and the world. All of your experiences went into making you the person you are today.

We present information in this book that we hope will help you to better understand yourself and the role you assumed in your family and continued into adulthood, in your personal life and at work. It is our hope that you will refer back to this book as a guide to implementing change in your life. Armed with the information and tools we have provided, you have the choice to stay on your present path or take a different one that may lead to greater professional success. We hope that through completing the various exercises, you have increased your awareness of the strengths you possess and the opportunities that exist as you acknowledge and utilize these strengths in all areas of your life.

Women have more options today than ever before. We are looking to make the most of the choices available, aware that, twenty to thirty years ago, other women worked to create a greater number of options from which women today may choose. Given the sheer number of alternatives, it is easy to feel overwhelmed and paralyzed by indecision. We need to take the time to identify the options and think through what is best for us as individuals, not exhaust ourselves by fretting over how hard it is to sift through such a vast amount of choices. It can be overwhelming, it can be frightening, or it can be an opportunity for fulfillment, happiness, and living the lives we want to live. Throw out the old rulebooks and "should's."

It is time to live life according to your own program, to identify your own wants and listen closely to your needs. If you focus solely on what will make you happy, that will help you find fulfillment and satisfaction. The only way to get to this place is to do the work of getting there. This means you must look inward and ask yourself the tough questions. How well is your life working for you? What do you need to do to improve the quality of your life? Would you like to try other ways of working and living? What are your professional goals? What steps do you need to take to achieve your goals?

As a woman, you can make your own choices. Although each of us once assumed one role or another, now is the time to determine whether the role you took on in your childhood is an appropriate one for the woman you are today and for the woman you wish to become. If you determine that you need to make changes in your life, then visualize the life you want. What elements of your visualized life are already in place? What must you do to turn this image into reality? It is important to remember that we are all constantly growing and going through different stages in our lives. Each new stage presents a myriad of possibilities for us to explore. Seize the opportunities.

You have the power and the right to change your life. We can do nothing to affect the past, but the future is like a blank canvas, waiting for you, the artist, to create a wonderful image: the person you have always wanted to become.

REFERENCES

Beck, A. T. *Cognitive Therapy and the Emotional Disorders.* New York: International Universities Press, 1976.

Bennis, W. "Four Competencies of Great Leaders." *Executive Excellence 5* (February 1988): 8–9.

Brown, I. C. Understanding Other Cultures. Englewood Cliffs, N.J.: Prentice-Hall, 1963.

Brown, L. M., and C. Gilligan. *Meeting at the Crossroads: Women's Psychology and Girls' Development.* Cambridge, Mass.: Harvard University Press, 1992.

Burke, R., and C. McKeen. "Mentoring in Organizations: Implications for Women." *Journal of Business Ethics 9* (1990): 317–32.

Freud, S. "Some physical consequences of the anatomical distinction between the sexes." In J. Starchey (ed.), *The Standard edition of the complete psychological works of Sigmund Freud,* vol. 19. London: Hogarth Press, 1925.

Grant, J. "Women as Managers: What They Can Offer to Organizations." *Organizational Dynamics* (1988): 56–63.

Miller, J. B. "The Development of Women's Sense of Self." In J. Jordan, A. Kaplan, J. B. Miller, I. Stiver, and J. Surrey (eds.), *Women's Growth in Connection: Writings from the Stone Center.* New York: The Guilford Press, 1991.

Moskal, B. "Women Make Better Managers." *Industry Week* 246, no. 3 (February 3, 1997): 17–20.

Noe, R. "Women and Mentoring: A Review and Research Agenda." *Academy of Management Review 13* (1988): 65–75.

Pfaff, L. A. *Five-Year Study Shows Gender Differences in Leadership Skills. APA Monitor 30* (1999).

Rosener, J. "Ways Women Lead." *Harvard Business Review* (November–December 1990): 119–25.

Ruderman, M., P. Ohlott, and K. Kram. "Promotional Decisions as a Diversity Practice." In K. S. McDonald and L. M. Hite (eds.), *Journal of Management Development 14,* no. 2 (1995) (Special issue: Gender Issues in Management Development): 6–23.

Schein, E. *Organizational Culture and Leadership: A Dynamic View.* San Francisco: Jossey-Bass, 1985.

Schein, E. "Organizational Culture." *American Psychologist 45* (1990): 109–19.

Stech, E. *Leadership Communication.* Chicago: Nelson-Hall, 1983.

Stiver, I. "Work Inhibitions in Women." In J. Jordan, A. Kaplan, J. B. Miller, I. Stiver, and J. Surrey (eds.), *Women's Growth in Connection: Writings from the Stone Center.* New York: The Guilford Press, 1991.

Surrey, J. "The Self-in-Relation: A Theory of Women's Development." In J. Jordan, A. Kaplan, J. B. Miller, I. Stiver, and J. Surrey (eds.), *Women's Growth in Connection: Writings from the Stone Center.* New York: The Guilford Press, 1991.

Tannen, D. *Talking from 9 to 5: How Women's and Men's Conversational Styles Affect Who Gets Heard, Who Gets Credit, and What Gets Done at Work.* New York: Morrow, 1994.

Wangensteen, B. "Take Out: Women in Business: Management Style: What's Gender Got to Do with It?" *Crain's New York Business,* September 29, 1997.

Wood, J. *Who Cares: Women, Care, and Culture.* Carbondale: Southern Illinois University Press, 1993.

Wood, J. *Gendered Lives: Communication, Gender, and Culture.* Belmont, Calif.: Wadsworth, 1994.

INDEX

aggressive communication, 146–147
assertive communication, 147

Beck, Aaron, 127–128
behaviors: beliefs and, 127; of Caregiver, 56–59, 65; changing of, 144–149; of Entrepreneur, 80–84, 87, 89; feminine, 104; learning of, 12–14; masculine, 104; of Maverick, 12, 32–35; modeling sources of, 13–14; of Peacekeeper, 20–22, 24–26, 26–29; of pleaser, 44–48, 54; self-assessment, 144; of Survivor, 68–71, 75–77
beliefs: accuracy assessments of, 134–136; assessment of, 133–134; changing of, 127–128; formation of, 126–127; negative, 128–129, 139; positive, 128; self-beliefs, 126–127, 133–134; thoughts identification and response exercise for analyzing. *see* thoughts identification and response exercise; verbal messages and, 126
Brown, Lyn Mikel, 13

Caregiver: behaviors of, 56–59, 65; case study examples of, 4, 8–9, 55–56, 59–62; changing behaviors of, 65, 144–149; characteristics of, 8–9, 56–57, 93; communication style of, 118–119; in corporate culture, 114; goals of, 92; leadership style of, 110; negative aspects of, 57; positive aspects of, 57, 65; self-concept of, 63; self-evaluative exercises, 57, 63–64; sensitivity of, 58–59, 96–97; strengths of, 57, 65, 94, 164; styles of, 59–62; traps of, 97–98; weaknesses of, 57, 95; workplace behaviors of, 56–59
change: of behaviors, 144–149; of beliefs, 127–128; for Caregiver, 65; Cognitive Therapy approach, 124–125, 127; criteria for success, 160–161; effecting of, 159; for Entrepreneur, 87, 89; leadership support of, 161; for Maverick, 41; organizational, 160–161; for Peacekeeper, 26–29; for Pleaser, 54; self-assessments, 125, 166; for Survivor, 75–77
Cognitive Therapy approach, 124–125, 127
communication: description of, 116; directive style of, 117; functions of, 117; man's approach, 117; tips for successful, 152; woman's approach, 116–117
communication style: aggressive, 146–147; assertive, 147; of Caregiver, 118–119; changing of, 146–147; description of, 118; of Entrepreneur, 119; of Maverick, 118; organizational, 119–120; of Peacekeeper, 118; of Pleaser, 118; self-assessment, 120–121; of Survivor, 119

corporate culture: Caregiver in, 114; characteristics of, 113–114, 161; description of, 113–114; elements of, 114; Entrepreneur in, 114–115; Maverick in, 114–115; Peacekeeper in, 114; Pleaser in, 114; self-assessment, 115–116; Survivor in, 114

culture. *see* corporate culture

development: gender differences in, 13; of roles, 11–12

Entrepreneur: behaviors of, 80–84, 87, 89; case study examples of, 5, 9–10, 79, 84–87; changing behaviors of, 87, 89, 144–149; characteristics of, 9–10, 79, 93; communication style of, 119; in corporate culture, 114–115; development of, 11; goals of, 92; leadership style of, 111; negative aspects of, 82; positive aspects of, 80; self-concept of, 87; self-evaluative exercises, 81, 87–88; sensitivity of, 82–84, 96–97; strengths of, 81, 94, 165; styles of, 84–87; traps of, 97–98; weaknesses of, 81, 95–96; workplace behaviors of, 80–84

family: modeling behaviors in, 13–14; role in, 15, 17; rules of, 15

future: change in organizations, 160–161; role assessments, 164–166; role models for, 161–162; strengths recognition, 162–166

gender: developmental differences, 13–14; leadership styles based on, 105–109; mentoring approaches, 153–154. *see also* men; women

Gilligan, Carol, 13

goals: Caregiver, 92; Entrepreneur, 92; Maverick, 92; Peacekeeper, 92; Pleaser, 92; setting of, 152; Survivor, 92

Imposter Syndrome: case study example of, 140; characteristics of, 139–140; definition of, 139; self-assessment, 141

leadership: change supported by, 161; characteristics of, 104–105; criteria for success, 105; relationships and, 107–108; stereotypes, 105; support and advisory group for, 112–113; women in, 105, 108–109

leadership style: of Caregiver, 110; of Entrepreneur, 111; gender differences, 105–109; of Maverick, 110; of Peacekeeper, 109; of Pleaser, 109–110; self-assessment of, 111–112; strategies for developing, 152; of Survivor, 110–111; woman's, 105

management: gender differences, 106–107; women in, 105–107

Maverick: behaviors of, 12, 32–35; case study examples of, 4, 7, 36–38; changing behaviors of, 41, 144–149; characteristics of, 7, 32–33, 40, 93; communication style of, 118; in corporate culture, 114–115; goals of, 92; leadership style of, 110; negative aspects of, 32; positive aspects of, 32; self-concept of, 38; self-evaluative exercises, 33, 39–40; sensitivity of, 34–35, 96–97; strengths of, 33, 94, 164; styles of, 36–38; traps of, 97–98; weaknesses of, 33, 95–96; workplace behaviors of, 32–35

men: development of, 13; modeling behaviors, 13–14

mentoring: benefits of, 155; definition of, 153; formal vs. informal relationship, 153; gender differences in, 153–154; programs, 154; self-assessments, 154–155

modeling: behaviors acquisition and, 13; definition of, 13; of men, 13–14; of women, 14

negative beliefs: description of, 128–129; self-doubts and, 139; workplace effects, 128–129

organization: changes to women-friendly atmosphere, 160–161; culture of. *see* corporate culture; environment of, 103–104; fit assessments, 155–158

Peacekeeper: behaviors of, 20–22, 24–26; changing behaviors of, 26–29, 144–149; characteristics of, 6, 19–20, 28, 93; communication
style of, 118; in corporate culture, 114; example of, 3–4, 6; goals of, 92; leadership style of,
109; negative aspects of, 20; positive aspects
of, 20; self-concept of, 26; self-evaluative
exercises, 21, 27–28; sensitivity of, 22–23,
96–97; strengths of, 20–21, 94, 164; styles of,
24–26; traps of, 97–98; weaknesses of, 21, 95;
workplace behaviors of, 20–22
Pleaser: behaviors of, 44–48; case study examples of, 4, 7–8, 43, 48–51; changing behaviors of, 54, 144–149; characteristics of, 7–8,
44–45, 53–54, 93; communication style of,
118; in corporate culture, 114; development of, 12; goals of, 92; insecurity of, 46,
51; leadership style of, 109–110; negative
aspects of, 44, 46; positive aspects of, 44;
self-concept of, 52; self-evaluative exercises,
45, 52–53; sensitivity of, 46–47, 96–97;
strengths of, 45, 54, 94, 164; styles of,
48–51; weaknesses of, 45, 95; workplace
behaviors of, 44–48
problem-solving strategies, 145–146

relationships: leadership and, 107–108; value
of, 160
role(s): Caregiver. see Caregiver; development
of, 11–12; Entrepreneur. see Entrepreneur;
familial, 15, 17; formation of, 11–12; identification of, 10–11, 99–100; Maverick. see
Maverick; Peacekeeper. see Peacekeeper;
Pleaser. see Pleaser; self-assessments, 10–11,
99–100, 124–125, 164–166; Survivor. see
Survivor; verbal messages effect, 12, 14;
workplace effects, 17
Rosener, Judy, 108

self-assessments: corporate culture, 115–116;
fit with organization culture and environment, 155–158; Imposter Syndrome, 141;
leadership style, 111–112; role, 10–11,
99–100, 124–125, 164–166; strengths, 136,
147, 162–163
self-care, 147–149
self-concept: assessments of, 133–139; of Caregiver, 63; definition of, 126, 132; of Entrepreneur, 87; of Maverick, 38; of Peacekeeper,
26; of Pleaser, 52; redefining process for,
133–139; self-esteem and, 132–133; of
Survivor, 74–75
self-confidence, 151
self-esteem: beliefs and, 127; definition of,
132; self-concept and, 132–133
self-management, 106
self-promotion: definition of, 149; exercise for
assessing, 151; factors that discourage,
149–150; self-confidence and, 151
strengths: of Caregiver, 57, 65, 94, 164; of Entrepreneur, 81, 94, 165; of Maverick, 33, 94, 164;
of Peacekeeper, 20–21, 94, 164; of Pleaser, 45,
54, 94, 164; recognizing of, 162–163; self-
assessments, 136, 147, 162–163; of Survivor,
69, 94, 164–165; of women, 107–108,
162–163
support and advisory group, 112–113
Survivor: behaviors of, 68–71, 75–77; case study
examples of, 4–5, 9, 67, 71–74, 84–87;
changing behaviors of, 75–77, 144–149;
characteristics of, 9, 67–69, 93; communication style of, 119; in corporate culture, 114;
goals of, 92; leadership style of, 110–111;
negative aspects of, 68; positive aspects of, 68;
self-concept of, 74–75; self-evaluative exercises, 69, 75–76; sensitivity of, 70–71, 96–97;
strengths of, 69, 94, 164–165; styles of,
71–74; traps of, 97–98; weaknesses of, 69, 95;
workplace behaviors of, 68–71

thoughts identification and response exercise:
case study example of, 131–132; components of, 129–130; purpose of, 128–129

verbal messages: beliefs and, 126; definition of, 12;
role formation and, 12, 14; in workplace, 15

weaknesses: of Caregiver, 57, 95; of Entrepreneur, 81, 95–96; of Maverick, 33, 95–96; of Peacekeeper, 21, 95; of Pleaser, 45, 95; of Survivor, 69, 95

women: development of, 13; in leadership roles, 105, 108–109; in management positions, 105–107; modeling behaviors of, 14; relationship and connectedness traits, 107; self-valuation by, 108–109; strengths of, 107–108. *see also* gender

workplace: Caregiver in, 56–59; culture of, 15; Entrepreneur in, 80–84; Maverick in, 32–35; negative beliefs effect, 128–129; Peacekeeper in, 20–22; Pleaser in, 44–48; rules of, 15; Survivor in, 68–71; verbal messages in, 15

Author Contact Information

Binnie Shusman Kafrissen and Fran Shusman are principals in The Delancey Group, a consulting firm specializing in organization development and change. The Delancey Group provides a variety of consulting services including workshops focusing on the development and retention of women, leadership development, team effectiveness, and career development. *Winning Roles for Career-Minded Women* is a valuable tool that can be used in conjunction with The Delancey Group's workshops.

If you would like more information, please contact the authors at the following address:

Binnie Shusman Kafrissen, Ph.D., & Fran Shusman, Ph.D.
c/o The Delancey Group
1550 Cherry Lane
Rydal, PA 19046
(215) 485-1441
thedelanceygroup.com